The Middle Class Gentleman

Moliere

Table of Contents

The Middle Class Gentleman

Moliere

Kessinger Publishing reprints thousands of hard–to–find books!

Visit us at http://www.kessinger.net

translated by Philip Dwight Jones

Comedy–Ballet presented at Chambord, for the entertainment of the
King, in the month of October 1670, and to the public in Paris for
the first time at the Palais–Royal Theater 23 November 1670

The Cast

Monsieur Jourdain, bourgeois.
Madame Jourdain, his wife.
Lucile, their daughter.
Nicole, maid.
Cleonte, suitor of Lucile.
Covielle, Cleonte's valet.
Dorante, Count, suitor of Dorimene.
Dorimene, Marchioness.
Music Master.
Pupil of the Music Master.
Dancing Master.
Fencing Master.
Master of Philosophy.
Tailor.
Tailor's apprentice.
Two lackeys.
Many male and female musicians, instrumentalists, dancers, cooks,
tailor's apprentices, and others necessary for the interludes.

The scene is Monsieur Jourdain's house in Paris.

ACT ONE

SCENE I (Music Master, Dancing Master, Musicians, and Dancers)

(The play opens with a great assembly of instruments, and in the middle of the stage is a pupil of the Music Master seated at a table composing a melody which Monsieur Jourdain has ordered for a serenade.)

MUSIC MASTER: (To Musicians) Come, come into this room, sit there and wait until he comes.

DANCING MASTER: (To dancers) And you too, on this side.

MUSIC MASTER: (To Pupil) Is it done?

PUPIL: Yes.

MUSIC MASTER: Let's see. . . This is good.

DANCING MASTER: Is it something new?

MUSIC MASTER: Yes, it's a melody for a serenade that I set him to composing here, while waiting for our man to awake.

DANCING MASTER: May I see it?

MUSIC MASTER: You'll hear it, with the dialogue, when he comes. He won't be long.

DANCING MASTER: Our work, yours and mine, is not trivial at present.

MUSIC MASTER: This is true. We've found here such a man as we both need. This is a nice source of income for us — this Monsieur Jourdain, with the visions of nobility and gallantry that he has gotten into his head. You and I should hope that everyone resembled him.

DANCING MASTER: Not entirely; I could wish that he understood better the things that we give him.

MUSIC MASTER: It's true that he understands them poorly, but he pays well, and that's what our art needs now more than anything else.

DANCING MASTER: As for me, I admit, I feed a little on glory. Applause touches me; and I hold that, in all the fine arts, it is painful to produce for dolts, to endure the barbarous opinions of a fool about my choreography. It is a pleasure, don't tell me otherwise, to work for people who can appreciate the fine points of an art, who know how to give a sweet reception to the beauties of a work and, by pleasurable approbations, gratify us for our labor. Yes, the most agreeable recompense we can receive for the things we do is to see them recognized and flattered by an applause that honors us. There is nothing, in my opinion, that pays us better for all our fatigue; and it is an exquisite delight to receive the praises of the well–informed.

MUSIC MASTER: I agree, and I enjoy them as you do. There is surely nothing more agreeable than the applause you speak of; but that incense does not provide a living. Pure praises do not provide a comfortable existence; it is necessary to add something solid, and the best way to praise is to praise with cash–in–hand. He's a man, it's true, whose insight is very slight, who talks nonsense about everything and applauds only for the wrong reasons but his money makes up for his judgments. He has discernment in his purse. His praises are in cash, and this ignorant bourgeois is worth more to us, as you see, than the educated nobleman who introduced us here.

DANCING MASTER: There is some truth in what you say; but I find that you lean a little too heavily on money; and material interest is something so base that a man of good taste should never show an attachment to it.

MUSIC MASTER: You are ready enough to receive the money our man gives you.

DANCING MASTER: Assuredly; but I don't place all my happiness in it, and I could wish that together with his fortune he had some good taste in things.

MUSIC MASTER: I could wish it too, that's what both of us are working for as much as we can. But, in any case, he gives us the means to make ourselves known in the world;

and he will pay others if they will praise him.

DANCING MASTER: Here he comes.

SCENE II (Monsieur Jourdain, Two Lackeys, Music Master, Dancing Master, Pupil, Musicians, and Dancers)

MONSIEUR JOURDAIN: Well gentlemen? What's this? Are you going to show me your little skit?

DANCING MASTER: How? What little skit?

MONSIEUR JOURDAIN: Well, the. . . What–do–you–call it? Your prologue or dialogue of songs and dances.

DANCING MASTER: Ha, ha!

MUSIC MASTER: You find us ready for you.

MONSIEUR JOURDAIN: I kept you waiting a little, but it's because I'm having myself dressed today like the people of quality, and my tailor sent me some silk stockings that I thought I would never get on.

MUSIC MASTER: We are here only to wait upon your leisure.

MONSIEUR JOURDAIN: I want you both to stay until they have brought me my suit, so that you may see me.

DANCING MASTER: Whatever you would like.

MONSIEUR JOURDAIN: You will see me fitted out properly, from head to foot.

MUSIC MASTER: We have no doubt of it.

MONSIEUR JOURDAIN: I had this robe made for me.

DANCING MASTER: It's very attractive.

MONSIEUR JOURDAIN: My tailor told me the people of quality dress like this in the mornings.

MUSIC MASTER: It's marvelously becoming.

MONSIEUR JOURDAIN: Hey lackeys! My two lackeys!

FIRST LACKEY: What do you wish, Sir?

MONSIEUR JOURDAIN: Nothing. I just wanted to see if you were paying attention. (To the two masters) What say you of my liveries?

DANCING MASTER: They're magnificent.

MONSIEUR JOURDAIN: (Half opening his gown, showing a pair of tight red velvet breeches, and a green velvet vest, that he is wearing) Here again is a sort of lounging dress to perform my morning exercises in.

MUSIC MASTER: It is elegant.

MONSIEUR JOURDAIN: Lackey!

FIRST LACKEY: Sir?

MONSIEUR JOURDAIN: The other lackey!

SECOND LACKEY: Sir?

MONSIEUR JOURDAIN: Hold my robe. (To the Masters) Do you think I look good?

DANCING MASTER: Very well. No one could look better.

MONSIEUR JOURDAIN: Now let's have a look at your little show. **MUSIC MASTER:** I would like very much for you to listen to a melody he (indicating his student)has just composed for the serenade that you ordered from me. He's one of my pupils who has an admirable talent for these kinds of things.

MONSIEUR JOURDAIN: Yes, but you should not have had that done by a pupil; you yourself were none too good for that piece of work.

MUSIC MASTER: You must not let the name of pupil fool you, sir. Pupils of this sort know as much as the greatest masters, and the melody is as fine as could be made. Just listen.

MONSIEUR JOURDAIN: (To Lackeys) Give me my robe so I can listen better . . . Wait, I believe I would be better without a robe. . . No, give it back, that will be better.

MUSICIAN: (Singing) I languish night and day, my suffering is extreme Since to your control your lovely eyes subjected me; If you thus treat, fair Iris, those you love, Alas, how would you treat an enemy?

MONSIEUR JOURDAIN: This song seems to me a little mournful, it lulls to sleep, and I would like it if you could liven it up a little, here and there.

MUSIC MASTER: It is necessary, Sir, that the tune be suited to the words.

MONSIEUR JOURDAIN: Someone taught me a perfectly pretty one some time ago. Listen . . . Now . . . how does it go?

DANCING MASTER: By my faith, I don't know.

MONSIEUR JOURDAIN: There are sheep in it.

DANCING MASTER: Sheep?

MONSIEUR JOURDAIN: Yes. Ah! (He sings) I thought my Jeanneton As beautiful as sweet; I thought my Jeanneton Far sweeter than a sheep. Alas! Alas! She is a hundred times, A thousand times, more cruel Than tigers in the woods! Isn't it pretty?

MUSIC MASTER: The prettiest in the world.

DANCING MASTER: And you sing it well.

MONSIEUR JOURDAIN: It's without having learned music.

MUSIC MASTER: You ought to learn it, Sir, as you are learning dancing. They are two arts which have a close connection.

DANCING MASTER: And which open the mind of a man to fine things.

MONSIEUR JOURDAIN: And do people of quality learn music, too?

MUSIC MASTER: Yes sir.

MONSIEUR JOURDAIN: I'll learn it then. But I don't know when I can find time; for besides the Fencing Master who's teaching me, I have also engaged a master of philosophy who is to begin this morning.

MUSIC MASTER: Philosophy is something; but music, sir, music . . .

DANCING MASTER: Music and dancing, music and dancing, that's all that's necessary.

MUSIC MASTER: There's nothing so useful in a State as music.

DANCING MASTER: There's nothing so necessary to men as dancing.

MUSIC MASTER: Without music, a State cannot subsist.

DANCING MASTER: Without the dance, a man can do nothing.

MUSIC MASTER: All the disorders, all the wars one sees in the world happen only from not learning music.

DANCING MASTER: All the misfortunes of mankind, all the dreadful disasters that fill the history books, the blunders of politicians and the faults of omission of great commanders, all this comes from not knowing how to dance.

MONSIEUR JOURDAIN: How is that?

MUSIC MASTER: Does not war result from a lack of agreement between men?

MONSIEUR JOURDAIN: That is true.

MUSIC MASTER: And if all men learned music, wouldn't that be a means of bringing about harmony and of seeing universal peace in the world?

MONSIEUR JOURDAIN: You are right.

DANCING MASTER: When a man has committed a mistake in his conduct, in family affairs, or in affairs of government of a state, or in the command of an army, do we not always say, "He took a bad step in such and such an affair?"

MONSIEUR JOURDAIN: Yes, that's said.

DANCING MASTER: And can taking a bad step result from anything but not knowing how to dance?

MONSIEUR JOURDAIN: It's true, you are both right.

DANCING MASTER: It makes you see the excellence and usefulness of music and the dance.

MONSIEUR JOURDAIN: I understand that, now.

MUSIC MASTER: Do you wish to see our pieces?

MONSIEUR JOURDAIN: Yes.

MUSIC MASTER: I have already told you that this is a little attempt I have made to show the different passions that music can express.

MONSIEUR JOURDAIN: Very good.

MUSIC MASTER (To musicians) Here, come forward. (To Monsieur Jourdain) You must imagine that they are dressed as shepherds.

MONSIEUR JOURDAIN: Why always as shepherds? You see nothing but that everywhere.

MUSIC MASTER: When we have characters that are to speak in music, it's necessary, for believability, to make them pastoral. Singing has always been assigned to shepherds; and it is scarcely natural dialogue for princes or merchants to sing their passions.

MONSIEUR JOURDAIN: Alright, alright. Let's see.

DIALOGUE IN MUSIC: (A Woman and Two Men)

ALL THREE: A heart, under the domination of love, Is always with a thousand cares oppressed. It is said that we gladly languish, gladly sigh; But, despite what can be said, There is nothing so sweet as our liberty!

FIRST MAN: There is nothing so sweet as the loving fires That make two hearts beat as one. One cannot live without amorous desires; Take love from life, you take away the pleasures.

SECOND MAN: It would be sweet to submit to love's rule, If one could find faithful love, But, alas! oh cruel rule! No faithful shepherdess is to be seen, And that inconstant sex, much too unworthy, Must renounce love eternally.

FIRST MAN: Pleasing ardor!

WOMAN: Happy liberty!

SECOND MAN: Deceitful woman!

FIRST MAN: How precious you are to me!

WOMAN: How you please my heart!

SECOND MAN: How horrible you are to me!

FIRST MAN: Ah, leave, for love, that mortal hate!

WOMAN: We can, we can show you a faithful shepherdess!

SECOND MAN: Alas! Where to find her?

WOMAN: In order to defend our reputation, I want to offer you my heart!

FIRST MAN: But, shepherdess, can I believe That it will not be deceitful?

WOMAN: We'll see through experience, Who of the two loves best.

SECOND MAN: Who lacks constancy, May the gods destroy!

ALL THREE: With ardors so beautiful Let us be inflamed! Ah, how sweet it is to love, When two hearts are faithful!

MONSIEUR JOURDAIN: Is that all?

MUSIC MASTER: Yes.

MONSIEUR JOURDAIN: I find it well–done, and there are some pretty enough sayings in it.

DANCING MASTER: Here, for my presentation, is a little display of the loveliest movements and the most beautiful attitudes with which a dance can possibly be varied.

MONSIEUR JOURDAIN: Are these shepherds too?

DANCING MASTER: They're whatever you please. Let's go! (Four dancers execute all the different movements and all the kinds of steps that the Dancing Master commands; and this dance makes the First Interlude.)

ACT TWO

SCENE I (Monsieur Jourdain, Music Master, Dancing Master, Lackeys)

MONSIEUR JOURDAIN: That's not all that bad, and those people there hop around well.

MUSIC MASTER: When the dance is combined with the music, it will have even better effect, and you will see something quite good in the little ballet we have prepared for you.

MONSIEUR JOURDAIN: That's for later, when the person I ordered all this for is to do me the honor of coming here to dine.

DANCING MASTER: Everything is ready.

MUSIC MASTER: However, sir, this is not enough. A person like you, who lives magnificently, and who are inclined towards fine things, should have a concert of music here every Wednesday or every Thursday.

MONSIEUR JOURDAIN: Is that what people of quality do?

MUSIC MASTER: Yes, Sir.

MONSIEUR JOURDAIN: Then I'll have them. Will it be fine?

MUSIC MASTER: Without doubt. You must have three voices— a tenor, a soprano, and a bass, who will be accompanied by a bass–viol, a theorbo, and a clavecin for the chords, with two violins to play the ritournelles.

MONSIEUR JOURDAIN: You must also add a trumpet marine. The trumpet marine is an instrument that pleases me and it's harmonious.

MUSIC MASTER: Leave it to us to manage things.

MONSIEUR JOURDAIN: At least, don't forget to send the musicians to sing at table.

MUSIC MASTER: You will have everything you should have.

MONSIEUR JOURDAIN: But above all, let the ballet be fine.

MUSIC MASTER: You will be pleased with it, and, among other things, with certain minuets you will find in it.

MONSIEUR JOURDAIN: Ah! Minuets are my dance, and I would like you to see me dance them. Come, my Dancing Master.

DANCING MASTER: A hat, sir, if you please. La, la, la, la. La, la, la, la. In cadence please. La, la, la, la. Your right leg. La, la, la, la. Don't move your shoulders so. La, la, la, la. Your arms are wrong. La, la, la, la. Raise your head. Turn the toe out. La, la, la, la. Straighten your body up.

MONSIEUR JOURDAIN: How was that? (Breathlessly)

MUSIC MASTER: The best.

MONSIEUR JOURDAIN: By the way, teach me how to bow to salute a marchioness; I shall need to know soon.

DANCING MASTER: How you must bow to salute a marchioness?

MONSIEUR JOURDAIN: Yes, a marchioness named Dorimene.

DANCING MASTER: Give me your hand.

MONSIEUR JOURDAIN: No. You only have to do it, I'll remember it well.

DANCING MASTER: If you want to salute her with a great deal of respect, you must first bow and step back, then bow three times as you walk towards her, and at the last one bow down to her knees.

MONSIEUR JOURDAIN: (After the Dancing Master has illustrated) Do it some. Good!

LACKEY: Sir, your Fencing Master is here. MONSIEUR JOURDAIN: Tell him to come in here for my lesson. I want you to see me perform.

SCENE II (Fencing Master, Music Master, Dancing Master, Monsier Jourdain, a Lackey)

FENCING MASTER: (After giving a foil to Monsieur Jourdain) Come, sir, the salute. Your body straight. A little inclined upon the left thigh. Your legs not so wide apart. Your feet both in a line. Your wrist opposite your hip. The point of your sword even with your shoulder. The arm not so much extended. The left hand at the level of the eye. The left shoulder more squared. The head up. The expression bold. Advance. The body steady. Beat carte, and thrust. One, two. Recover. Again, with the foot firm. Leap back. When you make a pass, Sir, you must first disengage, and your body must be well turned. One, two. Come, beat tierce and thrust. Advance. Stop there. One, two. Recover. Repeat. Leap back. On guard, Sir, on guard. (The fencing master touches him two or three times with the foil while saying, "On guard.")

MONSIEUR JOURDAIN: How was that? (Breathlessly)

MUSIC MASTER: You did marvelously!

FENCING MASTER: As I have told you, the entire secret of fencing lies in two things: to give and not to receive; and as I demonstrated to you the other day, it is impossible for you to receive, if you know how to turn your opponent's sword from the line of your body. This depends solely on a slight movement of the wrist, either inward or outward.

MONSIEUR JOURDAIN: In this way then, a man, without courage, is sure to kill his man and not be killed himself?

FENCING MASTER: Without doubt. Didn't you see the demonstration?

MONSIEUR JOURDAIN: Yes.

FENCING MASTER: And thus you have seen how men like me should be considered by the State, and how the science of fencing is more important than all the other useless sciences, such as dancing, music, ...

DANCING MASTER: Careful there, Monsieur swordsman! Speak of the dance only with respect.

MUSIC MASTER: I beg you to speak better of the excellence of music.

FENCING MASTER: You are amusing fellows, to want to compare your sciences with mine!

MUSIC MASTER: See the self–importance of the man!

FENCING MASTER: My little Dancing Master, I'll make you dance as you ought. And you, my little musician, I'll make you sing in a pretty way.

DANCING MASTER: Monsieur Clanger–of–iron, I'll teach you your trade.

MONSIEUR JOURDAIN: (To the Dancing Master) Are you crazy to quarrel with him, who knows tierce and quarte, and who can kill a man by demonstration?

DANCING MASTER: I disdain his demonstrations, and his tierce, and his quarte.

MONSIEUR JOURDAIN: Careful, I tell you.

FENCING MASTER: What? You little impertinent!

MONSIEUR JOURDAIN: Oh! My Fencing Master.

DANCING MASTER: What? You big workhorse!

MONSIEUR JOURDAIN: Oh! My Dancing Master.

FENCING MASTER: If I throw myself on you ...

MONSIEUR JOURDAIN: Careful.

DANCING MASTER: If I get my hands on you ...

MONSIEUR JOURDAIN: Be nice!

FENCING MASTER: I'll go over you with a curry–comb, in such a way...

MONSIEUR JOURDAIN: Mercy!

DANCING MASTER: I'll give you a beating such as ...

MONSIEUR JOURDAIN: I beg of you!

MUSIC MASTER: Let us teach him a little how to talk!

MONSIEUR JOURDAIN: Oh Lord! Stop.

SCENE III (Philosophy Master, Music Master, Dancing Master, Fencing Master, Monsieur Jourdain, Lackeys)

MONSIEUR JOURDAIN: Aha! Monsieur Philosopher, you come just in time with your philosophy. Come, make a little peace among these people.

PHILOSOPHY MASTER: What's happening? What's the matter, gentlemen.

MONSIEUR JOURDAIN: They have got into a rage over the superiority of their professions to the point of injurious words and of wanting to come to blows.

PHILOSOPHY MASTER: What! Gentlemen, must you act this way? Haven't you read the learned treatise that Seneca composed on anger? Is there anything more base and more shameful than this passion, which turns a man into a savage beast? And shouldn't reason be the mistress of all our activities?

DANCING MASTER: Well! Sir, he has just abused both of us by, despising the dance, which I practice, and music, which is his profession.

PHILOSOPHY MASTER: A wise man is above all the insults that can be spoken to him; and the grand reply one should make to such outrages is moderation and patience.

FENCING MASTER: They both had the audacity of trying to compare their professions with mine.

PHILOSOPHY MASTER: Should that disturb you? Men should not dispute amongst themselves about vainglory and rank; that which perfectly distinguishes one from the other is wisdom and virtue.

DANCING MASTER: I insist to him that dance is a science to which one cannot do enough honor.

MUSIC MASTER: And I, that music is something that all the ages have revered.

FENCING MASTER: And I insist to them that the science of fencing is the finest and the most necessary of all sciences.

PHILOSOPHY MASTER: And where then will philosophy be? I find you all very impertinent to speak with this arrogance in front of me, and impudently to give the name of science to things that one should not even honor with the name of art, and that cannot be classified except under the name of miserable gladiator, singer, and buffoon!

FENCING MASTER: Get out, you dog of a philosopher!

MUSIC MASTER: Get out, you worthless pedant!

DANCING MASTER: Get out, you ill–mannered cur!

PHILOSOPHY MASTER: What! Rascals that you are ... (The philosopher flings himself at them, and all three go out fighting).

MONSIEUR JOURDAIN: Monsieur Philosopher!

PHILOSOPHY MASTER: Rogues! Scoundrels! Insolent dogs!

MONSIEUR JOURDAIN: Monsieur Philosopher!

FENCING MASTER: A pox on the beast!

The Middle Class Gentleman

MONSIEUR JOURDAIN: Gentlemen!

PHILOSOPHY MASTER: Impudent rogues!

MONSIEUR JOURDAIN: Monsieur Philosopher!

DANCING MASTER: The devil take the jackass!

MONSIEUR JOURDAIN: Gentlemen!

PHILOSOPHY MASTER: Villains!

MONSIEUR JOURDAIN: Monsieur Philosopher!

MUSIC MASTER: To the devil with the impertinent fellow!

MONSIEUR JOURDAIN: Gentlemen!

PHILOSOPHY MASTER: Rascals! Beggars! Traitors! Impostors! (They leave).

MONSIEUR JOURDAIN: Monsieur Philosopher, Gentlemen! Monsieur Philosopher! Gentlemen! Monsieur Philosopher! Oh! Fight as much as you like. I don't know what to do, and I'll not spoil my robe to separate you. I would be a fool to go among them and receive some damaging blow.

SCENE IV (Philosophy Master, Monsieur Jourdain)

PHILOSOPHY MASTER: (Straightening the collar that indicates he is a Philosopher) Now to our lesson.

MONSIEUR JOURDAIN: Oh! Sir, I am distressed by the blows they gave you.

PHILOSOPHY MASTER: It's nothing. A philosopher knows how to take these things and I'll compose a satire against them, in the style of Juvenal, which will fix them nicely. Let it be. What would you like to learn?

MONSIEUR JOURDAIN: Everything I can, for I have every desire in the world to be educated, and I'm furious that my father and mother did not make me study all the sciences when I was young.

PHILOSOPHY MASTER: This is a reasonable sentiment. Nam sine doctrina vita est quasi mortis imago. You understand that, and you doubtless know Latin?

MONSIEUR JOURDAIN: Yes, but act as if I did not know it. Tell me what it says.

PHILOSOPHY MASTER: It says that without science life is almost an image of death.

MONSIEUR JOURDAIN: That Latin is right.

PHILOSOPHY MASTER: Don't you know some principles, some basics of the sciences?

MONSIEUR JOURDAIN: Oh yes! I can read and write.

PHILOSOPHY MASTER: Where would it please you for us to begin? Would you like me to teach you logic?

MONSIEUR JOURDAIN: What is this logic?

PHILOSOPHY MASTER: It is that which teaches the three operations of the mind.

MONSIEUR JOURDAIN: What are these three operations of the mind?

PHILOSOPHY MASTER: The first, the second, and the third. The first is to conceive well by means of the universals; the second is to judge well by means of the categories; and the third is to draw well a conclusion by means of figures. Barbara, Celarent, Darii, Ferio, Baralipton, etc.

MONSIEUR JOURDAIN: Those words are too ugly. This logic doesn't suit me at all. Let's learn something else that's prettier.

PHILOSOPHY MASTER: Would you like to learn morality?

MONSIEUR JOURDAIN: Morality?

PHILOSOPHY MASTER: Yes.

MONSIEUR JOURDAIN: What does it say, this morality?

PHILOSOPHY MASTER: It treats of happiness, teaches men to moderate their passions, and ...

MONSIEUR JOURDAIN: No, let's leave that. I'm as choleric as all the devils and there's no morality that sticks, I want to be as full of anger as I want whenever I like.

PHILOSOPHY MASTER: Would you like to learn physics?

MONSIEUR JOURDAIN: What's it about, this physics?

PHILOSOPHY MASTER: Physics explains the principles of natural things and the properties of the material world; it discourses on the nature of the elements, of metals, minerals, of stones, of plants and animals, and teaches the causes of all the meteors, the rainbow, the will o' the wisps, the comets, lightning, thunder, thunderbolts, rain, snow, hail, winds, and whirlwinds.

MONSIEUR JOURDAIN: There's too much commotion in it, too much confusion.

PHILOSOPHY MASTER: Then what do you want me to teach you?

MONSIEUR JOURDAIN: Teach me how to spell.

PHILOSOPHY MASTER: Very gladly.

MONSIEUR JOURDAIN: Afterwards, you may teach me the almanack, to know when there is a moon and when not.

PHILOSOPHY MASTER: So be it. Following your thought and treating this matter as a philosopher, it is necessary to begin according to the order of things, by an exact knowledge of the nature of letters and the different ways of pronouncing them all. And thereupon I must tell you letters are divided into vowels, called vowels because they express the voice; and into consonants because they sound with the vowels and only mark the diverse articulations of the voice. There are five vowels or voices: A, E, I, O, U.

MONSIEUR JOURDAIN: I understand all that.

PHILOSOPHY MASTER: The vowel A is formed by opening the mouth widely : A. Its vowels are to be given the sounds used in vocalizing: Ah–aye–ee–o–ou.

MONSIEUR JOURDAIN: A, A. Yes.

PHILOSOPHY MASTER: The vowel E is formed by approaching the lower jaw to the upper: A, E.

MONSIEUR JOURDAIN: A, E; A, E. By my faith, yes. Ah! How fine!
PHILOSOPHY MASTER: And the vowel I, by bringing the jaws still nearer each other and stretching the two corners of the mouth towards the ears: A, E, I.

MONSIEUR JOURDAIN: A, E, I. I. I. I. That's true. Long live science!

PHILOSOPHY MASTER: The vowel O is formed by opening the jaws and drawing together the two corners of the lips, upper and lower: O.

MONSIEUR JOURDAIN: O, O. There's nothing truer. A, E, I, O,I O.. That's admirable! I, O, I, O.

PHILOSOPHY MASTER: The opening of the mouth happens to make a little circle which represents an O.

MONSIEUR JOURDAIN: O, O, O. You are right! O. Ah! What a fine thing it is to know something!

PHILOSOPHY MASTER: The vowel U is formed by bringing the teeth nearly together without completely joining them, and thrusting the two lips outward, also bringing them nearly together without completely joining them: U.

MONSIEUR JOURDAIN: U, U. There's nothing truer. U.

PHILOSOPHY MASTER: Your two lips thrust out as if you were making a face, whence it results that if you want to make a face at someone and mock him, you have only to say to him "U."

MONSIEUR JOURDAIN: U, U. That's true. Ah! Why didn't I study sooner in order to know all that!

PHILOSOPHY MASTER: Tomorrow we shall look at the other letters, which are the consonants.

MONSIEUR JOURDAIN: Are there things as curious about them as about these?

PHILOSOPHY MASTER: Without a doubt. The consonant D, for example, is pronounced by clapping the tongue above the upper teeth: D.

MONSIEUR JOURDAIN: D, D, Yes. Ah! What fine things! Fine things!

PHILOSOPHY MASTER: The F, by pressing the upper teeth against the lower lip: F.

MONSIEUR JOURDAIN: F, F. That's the truth. Ah! My father and my mother, how I wish you ill!

PHILOSOPHY MASTER: And the R, by carrying the tip of the tongue to the top of the palate, so that being grazed by the air that comes out with force, it yields to it and comes back always to the same place, making a kind of trill: R. AR.

MONSIEUR JOURDAIN: R, R, AR. R, R, R, R, R, RA. That's true. Ah! What a clever man you are! And how I have lost time! R, R, R, AR.

PHILOSOPHY MASTER: I'll explain to you all these strange things to their very depths.

MONSIEUR JOURDAIN: Please do. But now, I must confide in you. I'm in love with a lady of great quality, and I wish that you would help me write something to her in a little note that I will let fall at her feet.

PHILOSOPHY MASTER: Very well.

MONSIEUR JOURDAIN: That will be gallant, yes?

PHILOSOPHY MASTER: Without doubt. Is it verse that you wish to write her?

MONSIEUR JOURDAIN: No, no. No verse.

PHILOSOPHY MASTER: Do you want only prose?

MONSIEUR JOURDAIN: No, I don't want either prose or verse.

PHILOSOPHY MASTER: It must be one or the other.

MONSIEUR JOURDAIN: Why?

PHILOSOPHY MASTER: Because, sir, there is no other way to express oneself than with prose or verse.

MONSIEUR JOURDAIN: There is nothing but prose or verse?

PHILOSOPHY MASTER: No, sir, everything that is not prose is verse, and everything that is not verse is prose.

MONSIEUR JOURDAIN: And when one speaks, what is that then?

PHILOSOPHY MASTER: Prose.

MONSIEUR JOURDAIN: What! When I say, "Nicole, bring me my slippers, and give me my nightcap," that's prose?

PHILOSOPHY MASTER: Yes, Sir.

The Middle Class Gentleman

MONSIEUR JOURDAIN: By my faith! For more than forty years I have been speaking prose without knowing anything about it, and I am much obliged to you for having taught me that. I would like then to put into a note to her: "Beautiful marchioness, your lovely eyes make me die of love," but I want that put in a gallant manner and be nicely turned.

PHILOSOPHY MASTER: Put it that the fires of her eyes reduce your heart to cinders; that you suffer night and day for her the torments of a . . .

MONSIEUR JOURDAIN: No, no, no. I want none of that; I only want you to say "Beautiful marchioness, your lovely eyes make me die of love."

PHILOSOPHY MASTER: The thing requires a little lengthening.

MONSIEUR JOURDAIN: No, I tell you, I want only those words in the note, but turned stylishly, well arranged, as is necessary. Please tell me, just to see, the diverse ways they could be put.

PHILOSOPHY MASTER: One could put them first of all as you said them: "Beautiful marchioness, your lovely eyes make me die of love." Or else: "Of love to die make me, beautiful marchioness, your beautiful eyes." Or else: "Your lovely eyes, of love make me, beautiful marchioness, die." Or else: "Die, your lovely eyes, beautiful marchioness, of love make me." Or else: "Me make your lovely eyes die, beautiful marchioness, of love."

MONSIEUR JOURDAIN: But, of all those ways, which is the best?

PHILOSOPHY MASTER: The way you said it: "Beautiful marchioness, your lovely eyes make me die of love."

MONSIEUR JOURDAIN: I never studied, and yet I made the whole thing up at the first try. I thank you with all my heart, and I ask you to come tomorrow early.

PHILOSOPHY MASTER: I shall not fail to do so. (He leaves).

MONSIEUR JOURDAIN: What? Hasn't my suit come yet?

THE LACKEY: No, Sir.

MONSIEUR JOURDAIN: That cursed tailor makes me wait all day when I have so much to do! I'm enraged. May the quartan fever shake that tormentor of a tailor! To the devil with the tailor! May the plague choke the tailor! If I had him here now, that detestable tailor, that dog of a tailor, that traitor of a tailor, I . . .

SCENE V (Master Tailor, Apprentice Tailor carrying suit, Monsieur Jourdain, Lackeys)

MONSIEUR JOURDAIN: Ah! You're here! I was getting into a rage against you.

MASTER TAILOR: I could not come sooner, and I put twenty men to work on your suit.

MONSIEUR JOURDAIN: You sent me some silk hose so small that I had all the difficulty in the world putting them on, and already there are two broken stitches.

MASTER TAILOR: They get bigger, too much so.

MONSIEUR JOURDAIN: Yes, if I always break the stitches. You also had made for me a pair of shoes that pinch furiously.

MASTER TAILOR: Not at all, sir.

MONSIEUR JOURDAIN: How, not at all!

MASTER TAILOR: No, they don't pinch you at all.

MONSIEUR JOURDAIN: I tell you, they pinch me.

MASTER TAILOR: You imagine that.

MONSIEUR JOURDAIN: I imagine it because I feel it. That's a good reason for you!

MASTER TAILOR: Wait, here is the finest court—suit, and the best matched. It's a masterpiece to have invented a serious suit that is not black. And I give six attempts to the best tailors to equal it.

MONSIEUR JOURDAIN: What's this? You've put the flowers upside down.

MASTER TAILOR: You didn't tell me you wanted them right side up.

MONSIEUR JOURDAIN: Did I have to tell you that?

MASTER TAILOR: Yes, surely. All the people of quality wear them this way.

MONSIEUR JOURDAIN: The people of quality wear the flowers upside down?

MASTER TAILOR: Yes, Sir.

MONSIEUR JOURDAIN: Oh! It's alright then.

MASTER TAILOR: If you like, I'll put them right side up.

MONSIEUR JOURDAIN: No, no.

MASTER TAILOR: You have only to say so.

MONSIEUR JOURDAIN: No, I tell you. You've made it very well. Do you think the suit is going to look good on me?

MASTER TAILOR: What a question! I defy a painter with his brush to do anything that would fit you better. I have a worker in my place who is the greatest genius in the world at mounting a rhinegrave, and another who is the hero of the age at assembling a doublet.

MONSIEUR JOURDAIN: The perruque and the plumes: are they correct?

MASTER TAILOR: Everything's good.

MONSIEUR JOURDAIN: (Looking at the tailor's suit) Ah! Ah! Monsieur Tailor, here's the material from the last suit you made for me. I know it well.

MASTER TAILOR: You see, the material seemed so fine that I wanted a suit made of it for myself.

The Middle Class Gentleman

MONSIEUR JOURDAIN: Yes, but you should not have cut it out of mine.

MASTER TAILOR: Do you want to put on your suit?

MONSIEUR JOURDAIN: Yes, give it to me.

MASTER TAILOR: Wait. That's not the way it's done. I have brought men to dress you in a cadence; these kinds of suits are put on with ceremony. Hey there! Come in, you! Put this suit on the gentleman the way you do with people of quality.

(Four APPRENTICE TAILORS enter, two of them pull off Monsieur Jourdain's breeches made for his morning exercises, and two others pull off his waistcoat; then they put on his new suit; Monsieur Jourdain promenades among them and shows them his suit for their approval. All this to the cadence of instrumental music.)

APPRENTICE TAILOR: My dear gentleman, please to give the apprentices a small tip.

MONSIEUR JOURDAIN: What did you call me?

APPRENTICE TAILOR: My dear gentleman.

MONSIEUR JOURDAIN: My dear gentleman! That's what it is to dress like people of quality! Go all your life dressed like a bourgeois and they'll never call you "My dear gentleman." Here, take this for the "My dear gentleman."

APPRENTICE TAILOR: My Lord, we are very much obliged to you.

MONSIEUR JOURDAIN: "My Lord!" Oh! Oh! "My Lord!" Wait, my friend. "My Lord" deserves something, and it's not a little word, this "My Lord." Take this. That's what "My Lord" gives you.

APPRENTICE TAILOR: My Lord, we will drink to the health of Your Grace.

MONSIEUR JOURDAIN: "Your Grace!" Oh! Oh! Oh! Wait, don't go. To me, "Your Grace!" My faith, if he goes as far as "Highness," he will have all my purse. Wait. That's for "My Grace."

APPRENTICE TAILOR: My Lord, we thank you very humbly for your liberality.

MONSIEUR JOURDAIN: He did well, I was going to give him everything. (The four Apprentice Tailors celebrate with a dance, which comprises the Second Interlude.)

ACT THREE

SCENE I (Monsieur Jourdain and his two Lackeys)

MONSIEUR JOURDAIN: Follow me, I am going to show off my clothes a little about town. And above all both of you take care to walk close at my heels, so people can see that you are with me.

LACKEYS: Yes, Sir.

MONSIEUR JOURDAIN: Call Nicole for me, so I can give her some orders. Don't bother, there she is.

SCENE II (Nicole, Monsieur Jourdain, two Lackeys)

MONSIEUR JOURDAIN: Nicole!

NICOLE: Yes, sir?

MONSIEUR JOURDAIN: Listen.

NICOLE: He, he, he, he, he!

MONSIEUR JOURDAIN: What are you laughing about?

NICOLE: He, he, he, he, he, he!

MONSIEUR JOURDAIN: What does the hussy mean by this?

NICOLE: He, he, he! Oh, how you are got up! He, he, he!

MONSIEUR JOURDAIN: How's that?

NICOLE: Ah! Ah! Oh Lord! He, he, he, he, he!

MONSIEUR JOURDAIN: What kind of little baggage is this? Are you mocking me?

NICOLE: Certainly not, sir, I should be very sorry to do so. He, he, he, he, he!

MONSIEUR JOURDAIN: I'll give you a smack on the nose if you go on laughing.

NICOLE: Sir, I can't help it. He, he, he, he, he, he!

MONSIEUR JOURDAIN: You are not going to stop?

NICOLE: Sir, I beg pardon. But you are so funny that I couldn't help laughing. He, he, he!

MONSIEUR JOURDAIN: What insolence!

NICOLE: You're so funny like that. He, he!

MONSIEUR JOURDAIN: I'll . . .

NICOLE: Please excuse me. He, he, he, he!

MONSIEUR JOURDAIN: Listen. If you go on laughing the least bit, I swear I'll give you the biggest slap ever given.

NICOLE: Alright, sir, it's done, I won't laugh any more.

MONSIEUR JOURDAIN: Take good care not to. Presently you must clean . . .

NICOLE: He, he!

MONSIEUR JOURDAIN: You must clean . . .

NICOLE: He, he!

MONSIEUR JOURDAIN: You must, I say, clean the room and . . .

NICOLE: He, he!

MONSIEUR JOURDAIN: Again! NICOLE: (Falling down with laughter) Then beat me sir, and let me have my laugh out, it will do me more good. He, he, he, he, he!

MONSIEUR JOURDAIN: I'm furious.

NICOLE: Have mercy, sir! I beg you to let me laugh. He, he, he!

MONSIEUR JOURDAIN: If I catch you . . .

NICOLE: Sir! I shall burst . . . Oh! if I don't laugh. He, he, he!

MONSIEUR JOURDAIN: But did anyone ever see such a hussy as that, who laughs in my face instead of receiving my, orders?

NICOLE: What would you have me do, sir?

MONSIEUR JOURDAIN: That you consider getting my house ready for the company that's coming soon, you hussy.

NICOLE: Ah, by my faith, I don't feel like laughing any more. All your guests make such a disorder here that the word "company" is enough to put me in a bad humor.

MONSIEUR JOURDAIN: Why, should I shut my door to everyone for your sake?

NICOLE: You should at least shut it to some people.

SCENE III (Madame Jourdain, Monsieur Jourdain, Nicole, Lackeys)

MADAME JOURDAIN: Ah, ah! Here's a new story! What's this, what's this, husband, this outfit you have on there? Don't you care what people think of you when you are got up like that? And do you want yourself laughed at everywhere?

MONSIEUR JOURDAIN: None but fools and dolts will laugh at me wife.

MADAME JOURDAIN: Truly, they haven't waited until now, your antics have long given a laugh to everyone.

MONSIEUR JOURDAIN: Who's everyone, if you please?

MADAME JOURDAIN: Everyone is everyone who is right and who is wiser than you. For my part, I am scandalized at the life you lead. I no longer recognize our house. One would say it's the beginning of Carnival here, every day; and beginning early in the morning, so it won't be forgotten, one hears nothing but the racket of fiddles and singers which disturbs the whole neighborhood.

NICOLE: Madame speaks well. I'll never be able to get my housework done properly with that gang you have come here. They have feet that hunt for mud in every part of town to bring it here; and poor Franoise almost has her teeth on the floor, scrubbing the boards that your fine masters come to dirty up every day.

MONSIEUR JOURDAIN: What, our servant Nicole, you have quite a tongue for a peasant.

MADAME JOURDAIN: Nicole is right, and she has more sense than you. I'd like to know what you think you're going to do with a Dancing Master, at your age?

NICOLE: And with a hulking Fencing Master who comes stamping his feet, shaking the whole house and tearing up all the floorboards in our drawing–room.

MONSIEUR JOURDAIN: Be quiet, both servant and wife!

MADAME JOURDAIN: Is it that you're learning to dance for the time when you'll have no legs to dance on?

NICOLE: Do you want to kill someone?

MONSIEUR JOURDAIN: Quiet, I tell you! You are ignorant women, both of you, and you don't know the advantages of all this.

MADAME JOURDAIN: You should instead be thinking of marrying off your daughter, who is of an age to be provided for.

MONSIEUR JOURDAIN: I'll think of marrying off my daughter when a suitable match comes along, but I also want to learn about fine things.

NICOLE: I heard said, Madame, that today he took a Philosophy Master to thicken the soup!

MONSIEUR JOURDAIN: Very well. I have a wish to have wit and to reason about things with decent people.

MADAME JOURDAIN: Don't you intend, one of these days, to go to school and have yourself whipped at your age?

MONSIEUR JOURDAIN: Why not? Would to God I were whipped this minute in front of everyone, if I only knew what they learn at school!

NICOLE: Yes, my faith! That would get you into better shape.

MONSIEUR JOURDAIN: Without doubt.

MADAME JOURDAIN: All this is very important to the management of your house.

MONSIEUR JOURDAIN: Assuredly. You both talk like beasts, and I'm ashamed of your ignorance. For example, do you know what are you speaking just now?

MADAME JOURDAIN: Yes, I know that what I'm saying is well said and that you ought to be considering living in another way.

MONSIEUR JOURDAIN: I'm not talking about that. I'm asking if you know what the words are that you are saying here?

MADAME JOURDAIN: They are words that are very sensible, and your conduct is scarcely so.

MONSIEUR JOURDAIN: I'm not talking about that, I tell you. I'm asking you: what is it that I'm speaking to you this minute, what is it?

MADAME JOURDAIN: Nonsense.

MONSIEUR JOURDAIN: No, no! That's not it. What is it we are both saying, what language is it that we are speaking right now?

MADAME JOURDAIN: Well?

MONSIEUR JOURDAIN: What is it called?

MADAME JOURDAIN: It's called whatever you want.

MONSIEUR JOURDAIN: It's prose, you ignorant creature.

MADAME JOURDAIN: Prose?

MONSIEUR JOURDAIN: Yes, prose. Everything is prose that is not verse; and everything that's not verse is prose. There! This is what it is to study! And you (to Nicole), do you know what you must do to say U?

NICOLE: What?

MONSIEUR JOURDAIN: Say U, in order to see.

NICOLE: Oh Well, U.

MONSIEUR JOURDAIN: What do you do?

NICOLE: I say U.

MONSIEUR JOURDAIN: Yes, but, when you say U, what do you do?

NICOLE: I do what you tell me to.

MONSIEUR JOURDAIN: Oh, how strange it is to have to deal with morons! You thrust your lips out and bring your lower jaw to your upper jaw: U, see? U. Do you see? I make a pout: U.

NICOLE: Yes, that's beautiful.

MADAME JOURDAIN: How admirable.

MONSIEUR JOURDAIN: But it's quite another thing, if you have seen O, and D, D, and F, F.

MADAME JOURDAIN: What is all this rigmarole?

NICOLE: What does all this do for us?

MONSIEUR JOURDAIN: It enrages me when I see these ignorant women.

MADAME JOURDAIN: Go, go, you ought to send all those people packing with their foolishness.

NICOLE: And above all, that great gawk of a Fencing Master, who ruins all my work with dust.

MONSIEUR JOURDAIN: Well! This Fencing Master seems to get under your skin. I'll soon show you how impertinent you are.(He has the foils brought and gives one to Nicole). There. Demonstration: The line of the body. When your opponent thrusts in quarte, you need only do this, and when they thrust in tierce, you need only do this. That is the way never to be killed, and isn't it fine to be assured of what one does, when fighting against someone? There, thrust at me a little, to see.

NICOLE: Well then, what? (Nicole thrusts, giving him several hits).

MONSIEUR JOURDAIN: Easy! Wait! Oh! Gently! Devil take the hussy!

NICOLE: You told me to thrust.

MONSIEUR JOURDAIN: Yes, but you thrust in tierce, before you thrust in quarte, and you didn't have the patience to let me parry.

MADAME JOURDAIN: You are a fool, husband, with all your fantasies, and this has come to you since you took a notion to associate with the nobility.

MONSIEUR JOURDAIN: When I associate with the nobility, I show my good judgment; and that's better than associating with your shopkeepers.

MADAME JOURDAIN: Oh yes, truly! There's a great deal to gain by consorting with your nobles, and you did so well with your fine Count you were so taken with!

MONSIEUR JOURDAIN: Peace! Think what you're saying. You know very well, wife, that you don't know who you're talking about, when you talk about him! He's a more important person than you think: a great Lord, respected at court, and who talks to the King just as I talk to you. Is it not a thing which does me great honor, that a person of this quality is seen to come so often to my house, who calls me his dear friend and treats me as if I were his equal? He has more regard for me than one would ever imagine; and, in front of everyone, he shows me so much affection that I am embarrassed myself.

MADAME JOURDAIN: Yes, he has a kindness for you, and shows his affection, but he borrows your money.

MONSIEUR JOURDAIN: So! Isn't it an honor for me to lend money to a man of that condition? And can I do less for a lord who calls me his dear friend?

MADAME JOURDAIN: And this lord, what does he do for you?

MONSIEUR JOURDAIN: Things that would astonish you if you knew them.

MADAME JOURDAIN: Like what?

MONSIEUR JOURDAIN: Blast! I cannot explain myself. It must suffice that if I have lent him money, he'll pay it back fully, and before long.

MADAME JOURDAIN: Yes. You are waiting for that.

MONSIEUR JOURDAIN: Assuredly. Didn't he tell me so?

MADAME JOURDAIN: Yes, yes, he won't fail to do it.

MONSIEUR JOURDAIN: He swore it on the faith of a gentleman.

MADAME JOURDAIN: Nonsense!

MONSIEUR JOURDAIN: Well! You are very obstinate, wife. I tell you he will keep his word, I'm sure of it.

MADAME JOURDAIN: And I'm sure he will not, and that all his show of affection is only to flatter you.

MONSIEUR JOURDAIN: Be still. Here he is.

MADAME JOURDAIN: That's all we needed! He's come again perhaps to borrow something from you. The very sight of him spoils my appetite.

MONSIEUR JOURDAIN: Be still, I tell you.

SCENE IV (Count Dorante, Monsieur Jourdain, Madame Jourdain, Nicole)

DORANTE: My dear friend, Monsieur Jourdain, how do you do?

MONSIEUR JOURDAIN: Very well, sir, to render you my small services.

DORANTE: And Madame Jourdain there, how is she?

MADAME JOURDAIN: Madame Jourdain is as well as she can be.

DORANTE: Well! Monsieur Jourdain, you are excellently well dressed!

MONSIEUR JOURDAIN: You see.

DORANTE: You have a fine air in that suit, and we have no young men at court who are better made than you.

MONSIEUR JOURDAIN: Well! well!

MADAME JOURDAIN: (Aside) He scratches him where it itches.

DORANTE: Turn around. It's positively elegant.

MADAME JOURDAIN: (Aside) Yes, as big a fool behind as in front.

DORANTE: My faith, Monsieur Jourdain, I was strangely impatient to see you. You are the man in the world I esteem most, and I was speaking of you again this morning in the bedchamber of the King.

MONSIEUR JOURDAIN: You do me great honor, sir. (To Madame Jourdain) In the King's bedchamber!

DORANTE: Come, put on . . .

MONSIEUR JOURDAIN: Sir, I know the respect I owe you.

DORANTE: Heavens! Put on your hat; I pray you, no ceremony between us.

MONSIEUR JOURDAIN: Sir . . .

DORANTE: Put it on, I tell you, Monsieur Jourdain: you are my friend.

MONSIEUR JOURDAIN: Sir, I am your humble servant.

DORANTE: I won't be covered if you won't.

MONSIEUR JOURDAIN: (Putting on his hat) I would rather be uncivil than troublesome.

DORANTE: I am in your debt, as you know.

MADAME JOURDAIN: Yes, we know it all too well.

DORANTE: You have generously lent me money upon several occasions, and you have obliged me with the best grace in the world, assuredly.

MONSIEUR JOURDAIN: Sir, you jest with me.

DORANTE: But I know how to repay what is lent me, and to acknowledge the favors rendered me.

MONSIEUR JOURDAIN: I have no doubt of it, sir.

DORANTE: I want to settle this matter with you, and I came here to make up our accounts together.

MONSIEUR JOURDAIN: There wife! You see your impertinence!

DORANTE: I am a man who likes to repay debts as soon as I can.

MONSIEUR JOURDAIN: (Aside to Madame Jourdain) I told you so.

DORANTE: Let's see how much do I owe you.

MONSIEUR JOURDAIN: (Aside to Madame Jourdain) There you are, with your ridiculous suspicions.

DORANTE: Do you remember well all the money you have lent me?

MONSIEUR JOURDAIN: I believe so. I made a little note of it. Here it is. Once you were given two hundred louis d'or.

DORANTE: That's true.

MONSIEUR JOURDAIN: Another time, six–score.

DORANTE: Yes. MONSIEUR JOURDAIN: And another time, a hundred and forty.

DORANTE: You're right.

MONSIEUR JOURDAIN: These three items make four hundred and sixty louis d'or, which comes to five thousand sixty livres.

DORANTE: The account is quite right. Five thousand sixty livres.

MONSIEUR JOURDAIN: One thousand eight hundred thirty–two livres to your plume–maker.

DORANTE: Exactly.

MONSIEUR JOURDAIN: Two thousand seven hundred eighty livres to your tailor.

DORANTE: It's true.

MONSIEUR JOURDAIN: Four thousand three hundred seventy–nine livres twelve sols eight deniers to your tradesman.

DORANTE: Quite right. Twelve sols eight deniers. The account is exact.

MONSIEUR JouRDAIN: And one thousand seven hundred forty–eight livres seven sols four deniers to your saddler.

DORANTE: All that is true. What does that come to?

MONSIEUR JOURDAIN: Sum total, fifteen thousand eight hundred livres.

DORANTE: The sum total is exact: fifteen thousand eight hundred livres. To which add two hundred pistoles that you are going to give me, which will make exactly eighteen thousand francs, which I shall pay you at the first opportunity.

MADAME JOURDAIN: (Aside) Well, didn't I predict it?

MONSIEUR JOURDAIN: Peace!

DORANTE: Will that inconvenience you, to give me the amount I say?

MONSIEUR JOURDAIN: Oh, no!

MADAME JOURDAIN: (Aside) That man is making a milk–cow out of you!

MONSIEUR JOURDAIN: Be quiet!

DORANTE: If that inconveniences you, I will seek it somewhere else.

MONSIEUR JOURDAIN: NO, Sir.

MADAME JOURDAIN: (Aside) He won't be content until he's ruined you.

MONSIEUR JOURDAIN: Be quiet, I tell you.

DORANTE: You have only to tell me if that embarrasses you.

MONSIEUR JOURDAIN: Not at all, sir.

MADAME JOURDAIN: (Aside) He's a real wheedler!

MONSIEUR JOURDAIN: Hush.

MADAME JOURDAIN: (Aside) He'll drain you to the last sou.

MONSIEUR JOURDAIN: Will you be quiet?

DORANTE: I have a number of people who would gladly lend it to me; but since you are my best friend, I believed I might do you wrong if I asked someone else for it.

MONSIEUR JOURDAIN: It's too great an honor, sir, that you do me. I'll go get it for you.

MADAME JOURDAIN: (Aside) What! You're going to give it to him again?

MONSIEUR JOURDAIN: What can I do? Do you want me to refuse a man of this station, who spoke about me this morning in the King's bedchamber?

MADAME JOURDAIN: (Aside) Go on, you're a true dupe.

SCENE V (Dorante, Madame Jourdain, Nicole)

DORANTE: You appear to be very melancholy. What is wrong, Madame Jourdain?

MADAME JOURDAIN: I have a head bigger than my fist, even if it's not swollen.

DORANTE: Mademoiselle, your daughter, where is she that I don't see her?

MADAME JOURDAIN: Mademoiselle my daughter is right where she is.

DORANTE: How is she getting on?

MADAME JOURDAIN: She "gets on" on her two legs.

DORANTE: Wouldn't you like to come with her one of these days to see the ballet and the comedy they are putting on at court?

MADAME JOURDAIN: Yes truly, we have a great desire to laugh, a very great desire to laugh.

DORANTE: I think, Madame Jourdain, that you must have had many admirers in your youth, beautiful and good humored as you were.

MADAME JOURDAIN: By Our Lady! Sir, is Madame Jourdain decrepit, and does her head already shake with palsy?

DORANTE: Ah! My faith, Madame Jourdain, I beg pardon. I did not remember that you are young. I am often distracted. Pray excuse my impertinence.

SCENE VI (Monsieur Jourdain, Madame Jourdain, Dorante, Nicole)

MONSIEUR JOURDAIN: There are two hundred louis d'or.

DORANTE: I assure you, Monsieur Jourdain, that I am completely yours, and that I am eager to render you a service at court.

MONSIEUR JOURDAIN: I'm much obliged to you.

DORANTE: If Madame Jourdain desires to see the royal entertainment, I will have the best places in the ballroom given to her.

MADAME JOURDAIN: Madame Jourdain kisses your hands [but declines].

DORANTE: (Aside to Monsieur Jourdain) Our beautiful marchioness, as I sent word to you, in my note, will come here soon for the ballet and refreshments; I finally brought her to consent to the entertainment you wish to give her.

MONSIEUR JOURDAIN: Let us move a little farther away, for a certain reason.

DORANTE: It has been eight days since I saw you, and I have sent you no news regarding the diamond you put into my hands to present to her on your behalf; but it's because I had the greatest difficulty in conquering her scruples, and it's only today that she resolved to accept it.

DORANTE: Marvelous. And I am greatly deceived if the beauty of that diamond does not produce for you an admirable effect on her spirit.

MONSIEUR JOURDAIN: Would to Heaven!

MADAME JOURDAIN: (To Nicole) Once he's with him he cannot leave him.

DORANTE: I made her value as she should the richness of that present and the grandeur of your love.

MONSIEUR JOURDAIN: These are, sir, favors which overwhelm me; and I am in the very greatest confusion at seeing a person of your quality demean himself for me as you do.

DORANTE: Are you joking? Among friends, does one stop at these sorts of scruples? And wouldn't you do the same thing for me, if the occasion offered?

MONSIEUR JOURDAIN: Oh! Certainly, and with all my heart.

MADAME JOURDAIN: (To Nicole) His presence weighs me down!

DORANTE: As for me, I never mind anything when it is necessary to serve a friend; and when you confided in me about the ardent passion you have formed for that delightful marchioness with whom I have contacts, you saw that I volunteered immediately to assist your love.

MONSIEUR JOURDAIN: It's true, these are favors that confound me.

MADAME JOURDAIN: (To Nicole) Will he never go?

NICOLE: They enjoy being together.

DORANTE: You took the right tack to touch her heart. Women love above all the expenses we go to for them; and your frequent serenades, your continual bouquets, that superb fireworks for her over the water, the diamond she has received from you, and the entertainment you are preparing for her, all this speaks much better in favor of your love than all the words you might have spoken yourself.

MONSIEUR JOURDAIN: There are no expenditures I would not make if by that means I might find the road to her heart. A woman of quality has ravishing charms for me and it's an honor I would purchase at any price.

MADAME JOURDAIN: (To Nicole) What can they talk about so much? Steal over and listen a little.

DORANTE: Soon enough you will enjoy at your ease the pleasure of seeing her, and your eyes will have a long time to satisfy themselves.

MONSIEUR JOURDAIN: To be completely free, I have arranged for my wife to go to dinner at her sister's, where she'll spend all the after–dinner hours.

DORANTE: You have done prudently, as your wife might have embarrassed us. I have given the necessary orders to the cook for you, and for the ballet. It is of my own invention; and, provided the execution corresponds to the idea, I am sure it will be found . . .

MONSIEUR JOURDAIN: (Sees that Nicole is listening, and gives her a slap) Say! You're very impertinent! (To Dorante) Let's go, if you please.

SCENE VII (Madame Jourdain, Nicole)

NICOLE: My faith, Madame, curiosity has cost me; but I believe something's afoot, since they were talking of some event where they did not want you to be.

MADAME JOURDAIN: Today's not the first time, Nicole, that I've had suspicions about my husband. I'm the most mistaken woman in the world, or there's some love–affair in the making. But let us see to my daughter. You know the love Cleonte has for her. He's a man who appeals to me, and I want to help his suit and give him Lucile, if I can.

NICOLE: Truly, Madame, I'm the most delighted creature in the world to see that you feel this way, since, if the master appeals to you, his valet appeals to me no less, and I could wish our marriage made under the shadow of theirs.

MADAME JOURDAIN: Go speak to Cleonte about it for me, and tell him to come to me soon so we can present his request to my husband for my daughter in marriage.

NICOLE: I hasten, Madame, with joy, for I could not receive a more agreeable commission. (Alone) I shall, I think, make them very happy.

SCENE VIII (Cleonte, Covielle, Nicole)

NICOLE: Ah! I'm glad to have found you. I'm an ambassadress of joy, and I come . . .

CLEONTE: Get out, traitor, and don't come to amuse me with your treacherous words.

NICOLE: Is this how you receive me . . .

CLEONTE: Get out, I tell you, and go tell your faithless mistress that she will never again in her life deceive the too trusting Cleonte.

NICOLE: What caprice is this? My dear Covielle, explain a little what you are trying to say.

COVIELLE: Your dear Covielle, little hussy? Go, quickly, out of my sight, villainess , and leave me in peace.

NICOLE: What! You come to me too. . . COVIELLE: Out of my sight, I tell you, and never speak to me again. NICOLE: My word! What fly has bitten those two? Let's go tell this pretty story to my mistress.

SCENE IX (Cleonte, Covielle)

CLEONTE: What! Treat a lover in this way? And a lover who is the most faithful and passionate of lovers?

COVIELLE: It is a frightful thing that they have done to us both.

CLEONTE: I show a woman all the ardor and tenderness that can be imagined; I love nothing in the world but her, and I have nothing but her in my thoughts; she is all I care for, all my desire, all my joy; I talk of nothing but her, I think of nothing but her, I have no dreams but of her, I breathe only because of her, my heart lives wholly in her; and see how so much love is well repaid! I have been two days without seeing her, which are for me two frightful centuries; I meet her by chance; my heart, at that sight, is completely transported, my joy shines on my face; I fly with ecstasy towards her — and the faithless one averts her eyes and hurries by as if she had never seen me in her life!

COVIELLE: I say the same things as you.

CLEONTE: Covielle, can one see anything to equal this perfidy of the ungrateful Lucile?

COVIELLE: And that, Monsieur, of the treacherous Nicole?

CLEONTE: After so many ardent homages, sighs, and vows that I have made to her charms!

COVIELLE: After so many assiduous compliments, cares, and services that I rendered her in the kitchen!

CLEONTE: So many tears I have shed at her knees!

COVIELLE: So many buckets of water I have drawn for her!

CLEONTE: So much passion I have shown her in loving her more than myself!

COVIELLE: So much heat I have endured in turning the spit for her!

CLEONTE: She flies from me in disdain!

COVIELLE: She turns her back on me!

CLEONTE: It is perfidy worthy of the greatest punishments.

COVIELLE: It is treachery that merits a thousand slaps.

CLEONTE: Don't think, I beg you, of ever speaking in her favor to me.

COVIELLE: I, sir? God forbid!

CLEONTE: Never come to excuse the action of this faithless woman.

COVIELLE: Have no fear.

CLEONTE; No, you see, all your speeches in her defense will serve no purpose.

COVIELLE: Who even thinks of that?

CLEONTE: I want to conserve my resentment against her and end all contact with her.

COVIELLE: I agree.

CLEONTE: This Count who goes to her house is perhaps pleasant in her view; and her mind, I well see, allows itself to be dazzled by social standing. But it is necessary for me, for my honor, to prevent the scandal of her inconstancy. I want to break off with her first and not leave her all the glory of dumping me. COVIELLE: That's very well said, and I agree, for my part, with all your feelings.

CLEONTE: Strengthen my resentment and aid my resolve against all the remains of love that could speak in her behalf. Tell me, I order you, all the bad you can of her; make for me a painting of her that will render her despicable; and show well, in order to disgust me, all the faults that you can see in her.

COVIELLE: Her, sir? There's a pretty fool, a well made flirt for you to give so much love! I see only mediocrity in her, and you will find a hundred women who will be more worthy of you. First of all, she has small eyes.

CLEONTE: That's true, she has small eyes; but they are full of fire, the brightest, the keenest in the world, the most touching eyes that one can see.

COVIELLE: She has a big mouth.

CLEONTE: Yes; but upon it one sees grace that one never sees on other mouths; and the sight of that mouth, which is the most attractive, the most amorous in the world, inspires desire.

COVIELLE: As for her figure, she's not tall.

CLEONTE: No, but she is graceful and well made.

COVIELLE: She affects a nonchalance in her speech and in her actions.

CLEONTE: That's true; but she may be forgiven all that, for her manners are so engaging, they have an irresistible charm.

COVIELLE: As to her wit . . .

CLEONTE: Ah! She has that, Covielle, the finest, the most delicate!

COVIELLE: Her conversation . . .

CLEONTE: Her conversation is charming.

COVIELLE: She is always serious . . .

CLEONTE; Would you have grinning playfulness, constant open merriment? And do you see anything more impertinent than those women who laugh all the time?

COVIELLE: But finally she is as capricious as any woman in the world.

CLEONTE: Yes, she is capricious, I concede; but everything becomes beautiful ladies well, one suffers everything for beauty.

COVIELLE: I see clearly how it goes, you want to go on loving her.

CLEONTE: Me, I'd like better to die; and I am going to hate her as much as I loved her.

COVIELLE: How, if you find her so perfect?

CLEONTE: That's how my vengeance will be more striking, in that way I'll show better the strength of my heart, by hating her, by quitting her, with all her beauty, all her charms, and as lovable as I find her. Here she is.

SCENE X (Cleonte, Lucile, Covielle, Nicole)

NICOLE: For my part, I was completely shocked at it.

LUCILE: It can only be, Nicole, what I told you. But there he is.

CLEONTE: I don't even want to speak to her.

COVIELLE: I'll imitate you.

LUCILE: What's the matter Cleonte? What's wrong with you?

NICOLE: What's the matter with you, Covielle?

LUCILE: What grief possesses you?

NICOLE: What bad humor holds you?

LUCILE: Are you mute, Cleonte?

NICOLE: Have you lost your voice, Covielle?

CLEONTE: Is this not villainous!

COVIELLE: It's a Judas!

LUCILE: I clearly see that our recent meeting has troubled you.

CLEONTE: Ah! Ah! She sees what she's done.

NICOLE: Our greeting this morning has annoyed you. **COVIELLE:** She has guessed the problem.

LUCILE: Isn't it true, Cleonte, that this is the cause of your resentment?

CLEONTE: Yes, perfidious one, it is, since I must speak; and I must tell that you shall not triumph in your faithlessness as you think, I want to be the first to break with you, and you won't have the advantage of driving me away. I will have difficulty in conquering the love I have for you; it will cause me pain; I will suffer for a while. But I'll come through it, and I would rather stab myself through the heart than have the weakness to return to you.

COVIELLE: Me too.

LUCILE: What an uproar over nothing. I want to tell you, Cleonte, what made me avoid joining you this morning.

CLEONTE: No, I don't want to listen to anything . . .

NICOLE: I want to tell you what made us pass so quickly.

COVIELLE: I don't want to hear anything.

LUCILE: (Following Cleonte) Know that this morning . . .

CLEONTE: No, I tell you.

NICOLE: (Following Covielle) Learn that . . .

COVIELLE: No, traitor.

LUCILE: Listen.

CLEONTE: I won't listen.

NICOLE: Let me speak.

COVIELLE: I'm deaf.

LUCILE: Cleonte! CLEONTE: No.

NICOLE: Covielle!

COVIELLE: I won't listen.

LUCILE: Stop.

CLEONTE: Gibberish!

NICOLE: Listen to me.

COVIELLE: Rubbish!

LUCILE: One moment.

CLEONTE: Never.

NICOLE: A little patience.

COVIELLE: Not interested!

LUCILE: Two words.

CLEONTE: No, you've had them.

NICOLE: One word.

COVIELLE: No more talking.

LUCILE: Alright! Since you don't want to listen to me, think what you like, and do what you want.

NICOLE: Since you act like that, make whatever you like of it all.

CLEONTE: Let us know the reason, then, for such a fine reception.

LUCILE: It no longer pleases me to say.

COVIELLE: Let us know something of your story.

NICOLE: I ,myself, no longer want to tell you.

CLEONTE: Tell me . . .

LUCILE: No, I don't want to say anything.

COVIELLE: Tell it . . .

NICOLE: No, I'll tell nothing.

CLEONTE: For pity . . .

LUCILE: No, I say.

COVIELLE: Have mercy.

NICOLE: It's no use.

CLEONTE: I beg you.

LUCILE: Leave me . . .

COVIELLE: I plead with you.

NICOLE: Get out of here.

CLEONTE: Lucile!

LUCILE: No.

COVIELLE: Nicole!

NICOLE: Never.

CLEONTE: In the name of God! . . .

LUCILE: I don't want to.

COVIELLE: Talk to me.

NICOLE: Definitely not.

CLEONTE: Clear up my doubts.

LUCILE: No, I'll do nothing.

COVIELLE: Relieve my mind!

NICOLE: No, I don't care to.

CLEONTE: Alright! since you are so little concerned to take me out of my pain and to justify yourself for the shameful treatment you gave to my passion, you are seeing me, ingrate, for the last time, and I am going far from you to die of sorrow and love.

COVIELLE: And I — I will follow in his steps.

LUCILE: Cleonte!

NICOLE: Covielle!

CLEONTE: What?

COVIELLE: Yes?

LUCILE: Where are you going?

CLEONTE: Where I told you.

COVIELLE: We are going to die.

LUCILE: You are going to die, Cleonte?

CLEONTE: Yes, cruel one, since you wish it.

LUCILE: Me! I wish you to die?

CLEONTE: Yes, you wish it.

LUCILE: Who told you that?

CLEONTE: Is it not wishing it when you don't wish to clear up my suspicions?

LUCILE: Is it my fault? And, if you had wished to listen to me, would I not have told you that the incident you complain of was caused this morning by the presence of an old aunt who insists that the mere approach of a man dishonors a woman — an aunt who constantly delivers sermons to us on this text, and tells us that all men are like devils we must flee?

NICOLE: There's the key to the entire affair.

CLEONTE: Are you sure you're not deceiving me, Lucile?

COVIELLE: Aren't you making this up?

LUCILE: There's nothing more true.

NICOLE: It's the absolute truth.

COVIELLE: Are we going to give in to this?

CLEONTE: Ah! Lucile, how with a word from your lips you are able to appease the things in my heart, and how easily one allows himself to be persuaded by the people one loves!

COVIELLE: How easily we are manipulated by these blasted minxes!

SCENE XI (Madame Jourdain, Cleonte, Lucile, Covielle, Nicole)

MADAME JOURDAIN: I am very glad to see you, Cleonte and you are here at just the right time. My husband is coming, seize the opportunity to ask for Lucile in marriage.

CLEONTE: Ah! Madame, how sweet that word is to me, and how it flatters my desires! Could I receive an order more charming, a favor more precious?

SCENE XII (Monsieur Jourdain, Madame Jourdain, Cleonte, Lucile, Covielle, Nicole)

CLEONTE: Sir, I did not want to use anyone to make a request of you that I have long considered. It affects me enough for me to take charge of it myself; and, without further ado, I will say to you that the honor of being your son—in—law is a glorious favor that I beg you to grant me.

MONSIEUR JOURDAIN: Before giving you a reply, sir, I beg to ask if you are a gentleman.

CLEONTE: Sir, most people don't hesitate much over this question. They use the word carelessly. They take the name without scruple, and the usage of today seems to validate the theft. As for me, I confess to you, I have a little more delicate feelings on this matter. I find all imposture undignified for an honest man, and that there is cowardice in disguising what Heaven made us at birth; to present ourselves to the eyes of the world with a stolen title; to wish to give a false impression. I was born of parents who, without doubt, held honorable positions. I have six years of service in the army, and I find myself established well enough to maintain a tolerable rank in the world; but despite all that I certainly have no wish to give myself a name to which others in my place might believe they could pretend, and I will tell you frankly that I am not a gentleman.

MONSIEUR JOURDAIN: Shake hands, Sir! My daughter is not for you.

CLEONTE: What?

MONSIEUR JOURDAIN: You are not a gentleman. You will not have my daughter.

MADAME JOURDAIN: What are you trying to say with your talk of gentleman? Are we ourselves of the line of St. Louis?

MONSIEUR JOURDAIN: Quiet, wife, I see what you are up to.

MADAME JOURDAIN: Aren't we both descended from good bourgeois families?

MONSIEUR JOURDAIN: There's that hateful word!

MADAME JOURDAIN: And wasn't your father a merchant just like mine?

MONSIEUR JOURDAIN: Plague take the woman! She never fails to do this! If your father was a merchant, so much the worse for him! But, as for mine, those who say that are misinformed. All that I have to say to you is, that I want a gentleman for a son-in-law.

MADAME JOURDAIN: It's necessary for your daughter to have a husband who is worthy of her, and it's better for her to have an honest rich man who is well made than an impoverished gentleman who is badly built.

NICOLE: That's true. We have the son of a gentleman in our village who is the most ill formed and the greatest fool I have ever seen.

MONSIEUR JOURDAIN: Hold your impertinent tongue! You always butt into the conversation. I have enough money for my daughter, I need only honor, and I want to make her a marchioness.

MADAME JOURDAIN: A marchioness?

MONSIEUR JOURDAIN: Yes, marchioness.

MADAME JOURDAIN: Alas! God save me from it!

MONSIEUR JOURDAIN: It's a thing I have resolved.

MADAME JOURDAIN: As for me, it's a thing I'll never consent to. Marriages above one's station are always subject to great inconveniences. I have absolutely no wish for a son-in-law who can reproach her parents to my daughter, and I don't want her to have children who will be ashamed to call me their grandmother. If she arrives to visit me in the equipage of a great lady and if she fails, by mischance, to greet someone of the neighborhood, they wouldn't fail immediately to say a hundred stupidities. "Do you see," they would say, "this madam marchioness who gives herself such glorious airs? It's the daughter of Monsieur Jourdain, who was all too glad, when she was little, to play house with us; she's not always been so haughty as she now is; and her two grandfathers sold cloth near St. Innocent's Gate. They amassed wealth for their children, they're paying dearly perhaps for it now in the other world, and one can scarcely get that rich by being honest." I certainly don't want all that gossip, and I want, in a word, a man who will be obliged to me for my daughter and to whom I can say, "Sit down there, my son-in-law, and have dinner with me."

MONSIEUR JOURDAIN: Surely those are the sentiments of a little spirit, to want to remain always in a base condition. Don't talk back to me: my daughter will be a marchioness in spite of everyone. And, if you make me angrier, I'll make a duchess of her.

MADAME JOURDAIN: Cleonte, don't lose courage yet. Follow me, my daughter, and tell your father resolutely that, if you can't have him, you don't want to marry anyone.

SCENE XIII (Cleonte, Covielle)

COVIELLE: You've made a fine business, with your pretty sentiments.

CLEONTE: What do you want? I have a scruple about that which precedent cannot conquer.

COVIELLE: Don't you make a fool of yourself by taking it seriously with a man like that? Don't you see that he is a fool? And would it cost you anything to accommodate yourself to his fantasies?

CLEONTE: You're right. But I didn't believe it necessary to prove nobility in order to be Monsieur Jourdain's son–in–law.

COVIELLE: Ha, ha, ha!

CLEONTE: What are you laughing at?

COVIELLE: At a thought that just occurred to me of how to play our man a trick and help you obtain what you desire.

CLEONTE: How?

COVIELLE: The idea is really funny.

CLEONTE: What is it?

COVIELLE: A short time ago there was a certain masquerade which fits here better than anything, and that I intend to make part of a prank I want to play on our fool. It all seems a little phony; but, with him, one can try anything, there is hardly any reason to be subtle, and he is the man to play his role marvelously and to swallow easily any fabrication we want to tell him. I have the actors, I have the costumes ready, just leave it to me.

CLEONTE: But tell me . . .

COVIELLE: I am going to instruct you in everything. Let's go, there he is, returning.

SCENE XIV (Monsieur Jourdain, Lackey) MONSIEUR JOURDAIN: What the devil is this? They have nothing other than the great lords to reproach me with, and as for me, I see nothing so fine as to associate with the great lords; there is only honor and civility among them, and I would have given two fingers of a hand to have been born a count or a marquis. LACKEY: Sir, here's the Count, and he has a lady with him. MONSIEUR JOURDAIN: What! My Goodness, I have some orders to give. Tell them I'll be back here soon.

SCENE XV (Dorimene, Dorante, Lackey)

LACKEY: Monsieur says that he'll be here very soon.

DORANTE: That's fine.

DORIMENE: I don't know, Dorante; I feel strange allowing you to bring me to this house where I know no one.

DORANTE: Then where would you like, Madame, for me to express my love with an entertainment, since you will allow neither your house nor mine for fear of scandal?

DORIMENE: But you don't mention that every day I am gradually preparing myself to receive too great proofs of your passion? As good a defense as I have put up, you wear down my resistance, and you have a polite persistence which makes me come gently to whatever you like. The frequent visits began, declarations followed, after them came serenades and amusements in their train, and presents followed them. I withstood all that, but you don't give up at all and step by step you are overcoming my resolve. As for me, I can no longer answer for anything, and I believe that in the end you will bring me to marriage, which I have so far avoided.

DORANTE: My faith! Madame, you should already have come to it. You are a widow, and you answer only to yourself. I am my own master and I love you more than my life. Why shouldn't you be all my happiness from today onward?

DORIMENE: Goodness! Dorante, for two people to live happily together both of them need particular qualities; and two of the most reasonable persons in the world often have trouble making a union satisfactory to them both.

DORANTE: You're fooling yourself, Madame, to imagine so many difficulties, and the experience you had with one marriage doesn't determine anything for others.

DORIMENE: Finally I always come back to this. The expenses that I see you go to for me disturb me for two reasons: one is that they get me more involved than I would like; and the other is that I am sure — meaning no offense — that you cannot do this without financially inconveniencing yourself, and I certainly don't want that.

DORANTE: Ah! Madame, they are trifles, and it isn't by that . . .

DORIMENE: I know what I'm talking about; and among other gifts, the diamond you forced me to take is worth ...

DORANTE: Oh! Madame, mercy, don't put any value on a thing that my love finds unworthy of you, and allow ... Here's the master of the house.

SCENE XVI (Monsieur Jourdain, Dorimene, Dorante, Lackey)

MONSIEUR JOURDAIN: (After having made two bows, finding himself too near Dorimene) A little farther, Madame.

DORIMENE: What?

MONSIEUR JOURDAIN: One step, if you please.

DORIMENE: What is it?

MONSIEUR JOURDAIN: Step back a little for the third.

DORANTE: Madame, Monsieur Jourdain is very knowledgeable.

MONSIEUR JOURDAIN: Madame, it is a very great honor to me to be fortunate enough to be so happy as to have the joy that you should have had the goodness to accord me the graciousness of doing me the honor of honoring me with the favor of your presence; and, if I also had the merit to merit a merit such as yours, and if Heaven . . . envious of my luck . . . should have accorded me . . . the advantage of seeing me worthy . . . of the . . .

DORANTE: Monsieur Jourdain, that is enough. Madame doesn't like grand compliments, and she knows that you are a man of wit. (Aside to Dorimene) As you can see, this good bourgeois is ridiculous enough in all his manners.

DORIMENE: It isn't difficult to see it.

DORANTE: Madame, he is the best of my friends.

MONSIEUR JOURDAIN: You do me too much honor.

DORANTE: A completely gallant man.

DORIMENE: I have great esteem for him.

MONSIEUR JOURDAIN: I have done nothing yet, Madame, to merit this favor.

DORANTE: (Aside to Monsieur Jourdain) Take care, nonetheless, to say absolutely nothing to her about the diamond that you gave her.

MONSIEUR JOURDAIN: Can't I even ask her how she likes it?

DORANTE: What? Take care that you don't. That would be loutish of you; and, to act as a gallant man, you must act as though it were not you who made her this present. (Aloud)

Monsieur Jourdain, Madame, says he is delighted to see you in his home.

DORIMENE: He honors me greatly.

MONSIEUR JOURDAIN: How obliged I am to you, sir, for speaking thus to her for me!

DORANTE: I have had frightful trouble getting her to come here.

MONSIEUR JOURDAIN: I don't know how to thank you enough.

DORANTE: He says, Madame, that he finds you the most beautiful woman in the world.

DORIMENE: He does me a great favor.

MONSIEUR JOURDAIN: Madame, it is you who does the favors, and . . .

DORANTE: Let's consider eating.

LACKEY: Everything is ready, sir.

DORANTE: Come then let us sit at the table. And bring on the musicians.

(Six cooks, who have prepared the feast, dance together and make the third interlude; after which, they carry in a table covered with many dishes.)

ACT FOUR

SCENE I (Dorimene, Monsieur Jourdain, Dorante, two Male Musicians, a Female Musician, Lackeys)

DORIMENE: Why, Dorante, that is really a magnificent repast!

MONSIEUR JOURDAIN: You jest, Madame; I wish it were worthy of being offered to you. (All sit at the table).

DORANTE: Monsieur Jourdain is right, Madame, to speak so, and he obliges me by making you so welcome. I agree with him that the repast is not worthy of you. Since it was I who ordered it, and since I do not have the accomplishments of our friends in this matter, you do not have here a very sophisticated meal, and you will find some incongruities in the combinations and some barbarities of taste. If Damis, our friend, had been involved, everything would have been according to the rules; everything would have been elegant and appropriate, and he would not have failed to impress upon you the significance of all the dishes of the repast, and to make you see his expertise when it comes to good food; he would have told you about hearth–baked bread, with its golden brown crust, crunching tenderly between the teeth; of a smooth, full–bodied wine, fortified with a piquancy not too strong, of a loin of mutton improved with parsley, of a cut of specially–raised veal as long as this, white and delicate, and which is like an almond paste between the teeth, of partridges complimented by a surprisingly flavorful sauce, and, for his masterpiece, a soup accompanied by a fat young turkey surrounded by pigeons and crowned with white onions mixed with chicory. But, as for me, I declare my ignorance; and, as Monsieur Jourdain has said so well, I only wish that the repast were more worthy of being offered to you.

DORIMENE: I reply to this compliment only by eating.

MONSIEUR JOURDAIN: Ah! What beautiful hands!

DORIMENE: The hands are mediocre, Monsieur Jourdain; but you wish to speak of the diamond, which is very beautiful.

MONSIEUR JOURDAIN: Me, Madame? God forbid that I should wish to speak of it; that would not be acting gallantly, and the diamond is a very small thing.

DORIMENE: You are very particular.

MONSIEUR JOURDAIN: You are too kind. . .

DORANTE: Let's have some wine for Monsieur Jourdain and for these gentlemen and ladies who are going to favor us with a drinking song.

DORIMENE: It is marvelous to season good food, by mixing it with music, and I see I am being admirably entertained.

MONSIEUR JOURDAIN: Madame, it isn't . .

DORANTE: Monsieur Jourdain, let us remain silent for these gentlemen and ladies; what they have for us to hear is of more value than anything we could say. (The male singers and the woman singer take the glasses, sing two drinking songs, and are accompanied by all the instrumental ensemble.)

FIRST DRINKING SONG Drink a little, Phyllis, to start the glass round. Ah! A glass in your hands is charmingly agreeable! You and the wine arm each other, And I redouble my love for you both Let us three — wine, you, and me — Swear, my beauty, to an eternal passion. Your lips are made yet more attractive by wetting with wine! Ah! The one and the other inspire me with desire And both you and it intoxicate me Let us three — wine, you, and me — Swear, my beauty, to an eternal passion.

SECOND DRINKING SONG Let us drink, dear friends, let us drink; Time that flies beckons us to it! Let us profit from life as much as we can. Once we pass under the black shadow, Goodbye to wine, our loves; Let us drink while we can, One cannot drink forever. Let fools speculate On the true happiness of life. Our philosophy Puts it among the wine–pots. Possessions, knowledge and glory Hardly make us forget troubling cares, And it is only with good drink That one can be happy. Come on then, wine for all, pour, boys, pour, Pour, keep on pouring, until they say, "Enough."

DORIMENE: I don't believe it's possible to sing better, and that is positively beautiful.

MONSIEUR JOURDAIN: I see something here, Madame, yet more beautiful.

DORIMENE: Aha! Monsieur Jourdain is more gallant than I thought.

DORANTE: What! Madame, what did you take Monsieur Jourdain for?

MONSIEUR JOURDAIN: I would like for her to take me at my word.

DORIMENE: Again!

DORANTE: You don't know him.

MONSIEUR JOURDAIN: She may know me whenever it pleases her.

DORIMENE: Oh! I am overwhelmed.

DORANTE: He is a man who is always ready with a repartee. But don't you see that Monsieur Jourdain, Madame, eats all the pieces of food you have touched?

DORIMENE: I am captivated by Monsieur Jourdain . . .

MONSIEUR JOURDAIN: If I could captivate your heart, I would be . . .

SCENE II (Madame Jourdain, Monsieur Jourdain, Dorimene, Dorante, Musicians, Lackeys)

MADAME JOURDAIN: Aha! I find good company here, and I see that I was not expected. Was it for this pretty affair, Monsieur Husband, that you were so eager to send me to dinner at my sister's? I just saw stage decorations downstairs, and here I see a banquet fit for a wedding. That is how you spend your money, and this is how you entertain the ladies in my absence, and you give them music and entertainment while sending me on my way.

DORANTE: What are you saying, Madame Jourdain? And what fantasies are you getting into your head that your husband spends his money, and that it is he who is giving this entertainment to Madame? Please know that it is I; that he only lends me his house, and that you ought to think more about the things you say.

MONSIEUR JOURDAIN: Yes, what impertinence. It is the Count who presents all this to Madame, who is a person of quality. He does me the honor of using my house and of wishing me to be with him.

MADAME JOURDAIN: All that's nonsense. I know what I know.

DORANTE: Come Madame Jourdain, put on better glasses.

MADAME JOURDAIN: I don't need glasses, sir, I see well enough; I have had suspicions for a long time, and I'm not a fool. This is very low of you, of a great lord, to lend a hand as you do to the follies of my husband. And you, Madame, for a great lady, it is neither fine nor honest of you to cause dissension in a household and to allow my husband to be in love with you.

DORIMENE: What is she trying to say with all this? Goodness Dorante! You have outdone yourself by exposing me to the absurd fantasies of this ridiculous woman.

DORANTE: Madame, wait! Madame, where are you going?

MONSIEUR JOURDAIN: Madame! Monsieur Count, make excuses to her and try to bring her back. Ah! You impertinent creature, this is a fine way to act! You come and insult me in front of everybody, and you drive from me people of quality.

MADAME JOURDAIN: I laugh at their quality.

MONSIEUR JOURDAIN: I don't know who holds me back, evil creature, from breaking your head with the remains of the repast you came to disrupt. (The table is removed).

MADAME JOURDAIN: (Leaving) I'm not concerned. These are my rights that I defend, and I'll have all wives on my side.

MONSIEUR JOURDAIN: You do well to avoid my rage. She arrived very inopportunely. I was in the mood to say pretty things, and I had never felt so witty. What's that?

SCENE III (Covielle, disguised; Monsieur Jourdain, Lackey)

COVIELLE: Sir, I don't know if I have the honor to be known to you?

MONSIEUR JOURDAIN: No, sir.

COVIELLE: I saw you when you were no taller than that.

MONSIEUR JOURDAIN: Me?

COVIELLE: Yes. You were the most beautiful child in the world, and all the ladies took you in their arms to kiss you.

MONSIEUR JOURDAIN: To kiss me?

COVIELLE: Yes, I was a great friend of your late father.

MONSIEUR JOURDAIN: Of my late father?

COVIELLE: Yes. He was a very honorable gentleman.

MONSIEUR JOURDAIN: What did you say?

COVIELLE: I said that he was a very honorable gentleman.

MONSIEUR JOURDAIN: My father?

COVIELLE: Yes.

MONSIEUR JOURDAIN: You knew him very well?

COVIELLE: Assuredly.

MONSIEUR JOURDAIN: And you knew him as a gentleman?

COVIELLE: Without doubt.

MONSIEUR JOURDAIN: Then I don't know what is going on!

COVIELLE: What?

MONSIEUR JOURDAIN: There are some fools who want to tell me that he was a tradesman.

COVIELLE: Him, a tradesman! It's pure slander, he never was one. All that he did was to be very obliging, very ready to help; and, since he was a connoisseur in cloth, he went all over to choose them, had them brought to his house, and gave them to his friends for money.

MONSIEUR JOURDAIN: I'm delighted to know you, so you can testify to the fact that my father was a gentleman.

COVIELLE: I'll attest to it before all the world.

MONSIEUR JOURDAIN: You'll oblige me. What business brings you here?

COVIELLE: Since knowing your late father, honorable gentleman, as I told you, I have traveled through all the world.

MONSIEUR JOURDAIN: Through all the world!

COVIELLE: Yes.

MONSIEUR JOURDAIN: I imagine it's a long way from here to there.

COVIELLE: Assuredly. I returned from all my long voyages only four days ago; and because of the interest I take in all that concerns you, I come to announce to you the best news in the world.

MONSIEUR JOURDAIN: What?

COVIELLE: You know that the son of the Grand Turk is here?

MONSIEUR JOURDAIN: Me? No.

COVIELLE: What! He has a very magnificent retinue; everybody goes to see it, and he has been received in this country as an important lord.

MONSIEUR JOURDAIN: By my faith! I didn't know that.

COVIELLE: The advantage to you in this is that he is in love with your daughter.

MONSIEUR JOURDAIN: The son of the Grand Turk?

COVIELLE: Yes. And he wants to be your son–in–law.

MONSIEUR JOURDAIN: My son–in–law, the son of the Grand Turk?

COVIELLE: The son of the Grand Turk your son–in–law. As I went to see him, and as I perfectly understand his language, he conversed with me; and, after some other discourse, he said to me, "Acciam croc soler ouch alla moustaph gidelum amanahem varahini oussere carbulath," that is to say, "Haven't you seen a beautiful young person who is the daughter of Monsieur Jourdain, gentleman of Paris?"

MONSIEUR JOURDAIN: The son of the Grand Turk said that of me?

COVIELLE: Yes. Inasmuch as I told him in reply that I knew you particularly well and that I had seen your daughter: "Ah!" he said to me, "marababa sahem;" Which is to say, "Ah, how I am enamored of her!"

MONSIEUR JOURDAIN: "Marababa sahem" means "Ah, how I am enamored of her"?

COVIELLE: Yes.

MONSIEUR JOURDAIN: By my faith, you do well to tell me, since, as for me, I would never have believed that "marababa sahem" could have meant to say "Oh, how I am enamored of her!" What an admirable language Turkish is!

COVIELLE: More admirable than one can believe. Do you know what Cacaracamouchen means?

MONSIEUR JOURDAIN: Cacaracamouchen? No.

COVIELLE: It means: It means, "My dear soul."

MONSIEUR JOURDAIN: Cacaracamouchen means "My dear soul?"

COVIELLE: Yes.

MONSIEUR JOURDAIN: That's marvelous! Cacaracamouchen, my dear soul. Who would have thought? I'm dumbfounded.

COVIELLE: Finally, to complete my assignment, he comes to ask for your daughter in marriage; and in order to have a father–in–law who should be worthy of him, he wants to make you a Mamamouchi, which is a certain high rank in his country.

MONSIEUR JOURDAIN: Mamamouchi?'

COVIELLE: Yes, Mamamouchi; that is to say, in our language, a Paladin. Paladin is one of those ancient . . . Well, Paladin! There is none nobler than that in the world, and you will be equal to the greatest lords of the earth.

MONSIEUR JOURDAIN: The son of the Grand Turk honors me greatly. Please take me to him in order to express my thanks.

COVIELLE: What! He is going to come here.

MONSIEUR JOURDAIN: He's coming here?

COVIELLE: Yes. And he is bringing everything for the ceremony of bestowing your rank.

MONSIEUR JOURDAIN: That seems very quick.

COVIELLE: His love can suffer no delay.

MONSIEUR JOURDAIN: All that embarrasses me here is that my daughter is a stubborn one who has gotten into her head a certain Cleonte, and she swears she'll marry no one but him.

COVIELLE: She'll change her mind when she sees the son of the Grand Turk; and then there is a remarkable coincidence here, it is that the son of the Grand Turk resembles this Cleonte very closely. I just saw him, someone showed him to me; and the love she has

68

for the one can easily pass to the other, and . . . I hear him coming. There he is.

SCENE IV (Cleonte, as a Turk, with three Pages carrying his outer clothes, Monsieur Jourdain, Covielle, disguised.)

CLEONTE: Ambousahim oqui boraf, Iordina, salamalequi.

COVIELLE: That is to say: "Monsieur Jourdain, may your heart be all the year like a flowering rosebush." This is the way of speaking politely in those countries.

MONSIEUR JOURDAIN: I am the most humble servant of His Turkish Highness.

COVIELLE: Carigar camboto oustin moraf .

CLEONTE: Oustin yoc catamalequi basum base alla moran.

COVIELLE: He says: "Heaven gives you the strength of lions and the wisdom of serpents."

MONSIEUR JOURDAIN: His Turkish Highness honors me too much, and I wish him all sorts of good fortune.

COVIELLE: Ossa binamen sadoc bahally oracaf ouram.

CLEONTE: Bel–men.

COVIELLE: He says that you should go with him quickly to prepare yourself for the ceremony; then you can see your daughter and conclude the marriage.

MONSIEUR JOURDAIN: So many things in two words?

COVIELLE: Yes; the Turkish language is like that, it says much in few words. Go quickly where he wants.

SCENE V (Dorante, Covielle)

COVIELLE: Ha, ha, ha! My faith, that was hilarious. What a dupe! If he had learned his role by heart, he could not have played it better. Ah! Ah! Excuse me, Sir, Wouldn't you like to help us here in an affair that is taking place.

DORANTE: Ah! Ah! Covielle, who would have recognized you? How you are made up!

COVIELLE: You see, ha, ha!

DORANTE: What are you laughing at?

COVIELLE: At a thing, Sir, that well deserves it.

DORANTE: What?

COVIELLE: I'll give you many chances, Sir, to guess the stratagem we are using on Monsieur Jourdain to get him to give his daughter to my master.

DORANTE: I can't begin to guess the stratagem, but I guess it will not fail in its effect, since you are undertaking it.

COVIELLE: I see, Sir, that you know me too well.

DORANTE: Tell me what it is.

COVIELLE: Come over here a little to make room for what I see coming. You can see part of the story, while I tell you the rest.

(The Turkish ceremony for ennobling Monsieur Jourdain is performed in dance and music, and comprises the Fourth Interlude.) [The ceremony is a burlesque full of comic gibberish in pseudo–Turkish and nonsensical French, in which Monsieur Jourdain is made to appear ludicrous and during which he is outfitted with an extravagant costume, turban, and sword.]

ACT FIVE

SCENE I (Madame Jourdaine, Monsieur Jourdain)

MADAME JOURDAIN: Ah, My God! Mercy! What is all of this? What a spectacle! Are you dressed for a masquerade, and is this a time to go masked? Speak then, what is this? Who has bundled you up like that?

MONSIEUR JOURDAIN: See the impertinent woman, to speak in this way to a Mamamouchi!

MADAME JOURDAIN: How's that?

MONSIEUR JOURDAIN: Yes, you must show me respect now, as I've just been made a Mamamouchi.

MADAME JOURDAIN: What are you trying to say with your Mamamouchi?

MONSIEUR JOURDAIN: Mamamouchi, I tell you. I'm a Mamamouchi.

MADAME JOURDAIN: What animal is that?

MONSIEUR JOURDAIN: Mamamouchi, that is to say, in our language, Paladin.

MADAME JOURDAIN: Baladin! Are you of an age to dance in ballets?

MONSIEUR JOURDAIN: What an ignorant woman! I said Paladin. It's a dignity which has just been bestowed upon me in a ceremony.

MADAME JOURDAIN: What ceremony then?

MONSIEUR JOURDAIN: Mahometa–per–Jordina.

MADAME JOURDAIN: What does that mean?

MONSIEUR JOURDAIN: Jordina, that is to say, Jourdain.

MADAME JOURDAIN: Very well, what of Jourdain?

MONSIEUR JOURDAIN: Voler far un Paladina de Jordina.

MADAME JOURDAIN: What?

MONSIEUR JOURDAIN: Dar turbanta con galera.

MADAME JOURDAIN: Which is to say what? MONSIEUR JOURDAIN: Per deffender Palestina.

MADAME JOURDAIN: What are you trying to say?

MONSIEUR JOURDAIN: Dara, dara, bastonnara.

MADAME JOURDAIN: What jargon is this?

MONSIEUR JOURDAIN: Non tener honta, questa star l'ultima affronta.

MADAME JOURDAIN: What in the world is all that?

MONSIEUR JOURDAIN: (Dancing and singing). Hou la ba, Ba la chou, ba la ba, ba la da.

MADAME JOURDAIN: Alas! Oh Lord, my husband has gone mad.

MONSIEUR JOURDAIN: (Leaving) Peace, insolent woman! Show respect to the Monsieur Mamamouchi.

MADAME JOURDAIN: Has he lost his mind? I must hurry to stop him from going out. Ah! Ah! This is the last straw! I see nothing but shame on all sides. (She leaves.)

Act FIVE

SCENE II (Dorante, Dorimene)

DORANTE: Yes, Madame, you are going to see the most amusing thing imaginable. I don't believe it would be possible to find in all the world another man as crazy as that one is. And then too, Madame, we must try to help Cleonte's plan by supporting his masquerade. He's a very gallant man and deserves our help.

DORIMENE: I think highly of him and he deserves happiness.

DORANTE: Besides that, we have here, Madame, another ballet performance that we shouldn't miss, and I want to see if my idea will succeed.

DORIMENE: I saw magnificent preparations, and I can no longer permit this Dorante. Yes, I finally want to end your extravagances and to stop all these expenses that I see you go to for me, I have decided to marry you right away. This is the truth of it, that all these sorts of things end with marriage, as you know.

DORANTE: Ah! Madame, is it possible that you should have taken such a sweet decision in my favor?

DORIMENE: It is only to impede you from ruining yourself; without that, I see very well that before long you would not have a penny.

DORANTE: How obliged I am to you, Madame, for the care you have to conserve my money! It is entirely yours, as well as my heart, and you may use them in whatever fashion you please.

DORIMENE: I'll make use of them both. But here is your man: his costume is wonderful.

SCENE III (Monsieur Jourdain, Dorante, Dorimene)

DORANTE: Sir, we come to pay homage, Madame and I, to your new dignity, and to rejoice with you at the marriage between your daughter and the son of the Grand Turk.

MONSIEUR JOURDAIN: (After bowing in the Turkish way) Sir, I wish you the strength of serpents and the wisdom of lions.

DORIMENE,: I was very glad, Sir, to be among the first to come to congratulate you upon rising to such a high degree of honor.

MONSIEUR JOURDAIN: Madame, I wish your rosebush to flower all year long; I am infinitely obliged to you for taking part in the honors bestowed upon me; and I am very happy to see you returned here, so I can make very humble excuses for the ridiculous behavior of my wife.

DORIMENE: That's nothing. I excuse her jumping to conclusions: your heart must be precious to her, and it isn't strange that the possession of such a man as you should inspire some jealousy.

MONSIEUR JOURDAIN: The possession of my heart is a thing that has been entirely gained by you.

DORANTE: You see, Madame, that Monsieur Jourdain is not one of those men that good fortune blinds, and that he still knows, even in his glory, how to recognize his friends.

DORIMENE: It is the mark of a completely generous soul.

DORANTE: Where then is His Turkish Highness? We want, as your friends, to pay him our respects.

MONSIEUR JOURDAIN: There he comes, and I have sent for my daughter in order to give him her hand.

SCENE IV (Cleonte, Covielle, Monsieur Jourdain, etc.)

DORANTE: Sir, we come to bow to Your Highness as friends of the gentleman who is your father–in–law, and to assure you with respect of our very humble services.

MONSIEUR JOURDAIN: Where's the interpreter to tell him who you are and to make him understand what you say? You will see that he will reply, and that he speaks Turkish marvelously. Hey there! Where the devil has he gone? (To Cleonte). Strouf, strif, strof, straf. The gentleman is a grande Segnore, grande Segnore, grande Segnore. And Madame is a Dama granda Dama, granda. Ahi! He, Monsieur, he French Mamamauchi, and Madame also French Mamamouchie. I can't say it more clearly. Good, here's the interpreter. Where are you going? We won't know how to say anything without you. Tell him, that Monsieur and Madame are persons of high rank, who have come to pay their respects to him, as my friends, and to assure him of their services. You'll see how he will reply.

COVIELLE: Alabala crociam acci boram alabamen.

CLEONTE: Catalequi tubal ourin soter amalouchan.

MONSIEUR JOURDAIN: See?

COVIELLE: He says that the rain of prosperity should water the garden of your family in all seasons.

MONSIEUR JOURDAIN: I told you that he speaks Turkish!

DORANTE: That's wonderful.

SCENE V (Lucile, Monsieur Jourdain, Dorante, Dorimene, etc.)

MONSIEUR JOURDAIN: Come, my daughter; come here and give your hand to the gentleman who does you the honor of asking for you in marriage.

LUCILE: What! Father, look at you! Are you playing in a comedy?

MONSIEUR JOURDAIN: No, no, this is not a comedy, it's a very serious matter, and as full of honor for you as possible. There is the husband I give you.

LUCILE: To me, father?

MONSIEUR JOURDAIN: Yes, to you. Come, put your hand in his, and give thanks to Heaven for your happiness.

LUCILE: I have absolutely no wish to marry.

MONSIEUR JOURDAIN: I wish it, I, who am your father.

LUCILLE: I'll do nothing of the sort.

MONSIEUR JOURDAIN: Ah! What a nuisance! Come, I tell you. Give your hand.

LUCILE: No, my father, I told you, there is no power on earth that can make me take any husband other than Cleonte. And I will go to extreme measures rather than . . . (Recognizes Cleonte) It is true that you are my father; I owe you complete obedience; and it is for you to dispose of me according to your wishes.

MONSIEUR JOURDAIN: Ah! I am delighted to see you return so promptly to your duty, and it pleases me to have an obedient daughter.

SCENE VI (Madame Jourdain, Monsieur Jourdain, Cleonte, etc.)

MADAME JOURDAIN: What now? What's this? They say that you want to give your daughter in marriage to a someone in a Carnival costume?

MONSIEUR JOURDAIN: Will you be quiet, impertinent woman? You always throw your absurdities into everything, and there's no teaching you to be reasonable.

MADAME JOURDAIN: It's you that there is no way of making wise, and you go from folly to folly. What is your plan, and what do you want to do with this assemblage of people?

MONSIEUR JOURDAIN: I want to marry our daughter to the son of the Grand Turk.

MADAME JOURDAIN: To the son of the Grand Turk?

MONSIEUR JOURDAIN: Yes. Greet him through the interpreter there.

MADAME JOURDAIN: I don't need an interpreter; and I'll tell him straight out myself, to his face, that there is no way he will have my daughter.

MONSIEUR JOURDAIN: I ask again, will you be quiet?

DORANTE: What! Madame Jourdain, do you oppose such good fortune as that? You refuse His Turkish Highness as your son–in–law?

MADAME JOURDAIN: My Goodness, Sir, mind your own business.

DORIMENE: It's a great glory, which is not to be rejected.

MADAME JOURDAIN: Madame, I beg you also not to concern yourself with what does not affect you.

DORANTE: It's the friendship we have for you that makes us involve ourselves in your interest.

MADAME JOURDAIN: I can get along quite well without your friendship.

DORANTE: Your daughter here agrees to the wishes of her father.

MADAME JOURDAIN: My daughter consents to marry a Turk?

DORANTE: Without doubt.

MADAME JOURDAIN: She can forget Cleonte?

DORANTE: What wouldn't one do to be a great lady?

MADAME JOURDAIN: I would strangle her with my own hands if she did something like that.

MONSIEUR JOURDAIN: That is just so much talk. I tell you, this marriage shall take place.

MADAME JOURDAIN: And I say there is no way that it will happen.

MONSIEUR JOURDAIN: Oh, what a row!

LUCILE: Mother!

MADAME JOURDAIN: Go away, you are a hussy.

MONSIEUR JOURDAIN: What! You quarrel with her for obeying me?

MADAME JOURDAIN: Yes. She is mine as much as yours.

COVIELLE: Madame!

MADAME JOURDAIN: What do you want to tell me?

COVIELLE: A word.

MADAME JOURDAIN: I want nothing to do with your word.

COVIELLE: (To Monsieur Jourdain) Sir, if she will hear a word in private, I promise you to make her consent to what you want.

MADAME JOURDAIN: I will never consent to it.

COVIELLE: Only listen to me.

MADAME JOURDAIN: No.

MONSIEUR JOURDAIN: Listen to him.

MADAME JOURDAIN: No, I don't want to listen to him.

MONSIEUR JOURDAIN: He is going tell you . . .

MADAME JOURDAIN: I don't want him to tell me anything whatsoever.

MONSIEUR JOURDAIN: There is the great stubbornness of a woman! How can it hurt you to listen to him?

COVIELLE: Just listen to me; after that you can do as you please.

MADAME JOURDAIN: Alright! What?

COVIELLE: (Aside to Madame Jourdain) For an hour, Madame, we've been signaling to you. Don't you see that all this is done only to accommodate ourselves to the fantasies of your husband, that we are fooling him under this disguise and that it is Cleonte himself who is the son of the Grand Turk? MADAME JOURDAIN: Ah! Ah! COVIELLE: And I, Covielle, am the interpreter? MADAME JOURDAIN: Ah! If this is the case then, I surrender.

COVIELLE: Don't let on.

MADAME JOURDAIN: Yes, it's done, I agree to the marriage.

MONSIEUR JOURDAIN: Ah! Now everyone's reasonable. You didn't want to hear it. I knew he would explain to you what it means to be the son of the Grand Turk.

MADAME JOURDAIN: He explained it to me very well, and I am satisfied. Let us send for a notary.

DORANTE: This is very well said. And finally, Madame Jourdain, in order to relieve your mind completely, and that you may lose today all the jealousy that you may have conceived of your husband, we shall have the same notary marry us, Madame and me.

MADAME JOURDAIN: I agree to that also.

MONSIEUR JOURDAIN: Is this to make her believe our story?

DORANTE: (Aside to Monsieur Jourdain) It is necessary to amuse her with this pretence.

MONSIEUR JOURDAIN: Good, good! Someone go for the notary.

DORANTE: While we wait for him to come and while he draws up the contracts, let us see our ballet, and divert His Turkish Highness with it.

MONSIEUR JOURDAIN: That is very well advised. Come, let's take our places.

MADAME JOURDAIN: And Nicole?

MONSIEUR JOURDAIN: I give her to the interpreter; and my wife to whoever wants her.

COVIELLE: Sir, I thank you. (Aside) If one can find a greater fool, I'll go to Rome to tell it.

(The comedy ends with a ballet.)